Conversations with Jerome Charyn

Literary Conversations Series
Peggy Whitman Prenshaw
General Editor

Conversations
with Jerome Charyn

Edited by Sophie Vallas

University Press of Mississippi   *Jackson*

www.upress.state.ms.us

The University Press of Mississippi is a member
of the Association of American University Presses.

Published with the help of the LERMA Research Center (EA 853),
at Aix-Marseille University.

First printing 2014

∞

Library of Congress Cataloging-in-Publication Data

Conversations with Jerome Charyn / edited by Sophie Vallas.
     pages cm. — (Literary conversations series)
   Includes index.
   ISBN 978-1-62846-089-6 (cloth : alk. paper) — ISBN 978-1-62846-090-2
(ebook) 1. Charyn, Jerome—Interviews. 2. Novelists, American—20th
century—Interviews. I. Vallas, Sophie, editor of compilation.
   PS3553.H33Z46 2014
   813'.54—dc23
   [B]   2014001980

British Library Cataloging-in-Publication Data available

Books by Jerome Charyn

(First American editions, first French editions with their existing American translations, and books published only in French)

Fiction

Once upon a Droshky. New York: McGraw-Hill, 1964.
On the Darkening Green. New York: McGraw-Hill, 1965.
The Man Who Grew Younger and Other Stories. New York: Harper and Row, 1967.
Going to Jerusalem. New York: The Viking Press, 1967.
American Scrapbook. New York: The Viking Press, 1969.
Eisenhower, My Eisenhower. New York: Holt, Rinehart and Winston, 1971.
The Tar Baby. New York: Holt, Rinehart and Winston, 1973.
The Franklin Scare. New York: Arbor House, 1977.
The Seventh Babe. New York: Arbor House, 1979.
The Catfish Man: A Conjured Life. New York: Arbor House, 1980.
Darlin' Bill: A Love Story of the Wild West. New York: Arbor House, 1980.
Panna Maria. New York: Arbor House, 1982.
Pinocchio's Nose. New York: Arbor House, 1983.
War Cries over Avenue C. New York: Donald I. Fine, 1985.
Captain Kidd. New York: St Martin's Press, 1999.
The Green Lantern: A Romance of Stalinist Russia. New York: Thunder's Mouth Press, 2004.
Johnny One-Eye: A Tale of the American Revolution. New York: Norton, 2008.
The Secret Life of Emily Dickinson: A Novel. New York: Norton, 2010.
Jerzy Kosinski. Translated by Bernard Hœpffner. Paris: Denoël, 2011.

Crime fiction

Blue Eyes. New York: Simon and Schuster, 1974.

Marilyn the Wild. New York: Arbor House, 1976.
The Education of Patrick Silver. New York: Arbor House, 1976.
Secret Isaac. New York: Arbor House, 1978.
Arnold, le geek de New York. With Michel Martens. Paris: Libération, 1980.
The Isaac Quartet (Blue Eyes, Marilyn the Wild, The Education of Patrick Silver, Secret Isaac). London: Zomba Books, 1984 [republished New York: Four Walls Eight Windows, 2002].
Paradise Man. New York: Donald I. Fine, 1987.
The Good Policeman. New York: The Mysterious Press, 1990.
Elsinore. New York: The Mysterious Press, 1991.
Maria's Girls. New York: The Mysterious Press, 1992.
Montezuma's Man. New York: The Mysterious Press, 1993.
Little Angel Street. New York: The Mysterious Press, 1994.
El Bronx. New York: The Mysterious Press, 1997.
Death of a Tango King. New York: New York University Press, 1998.
Sinbad. Drawings by Paul Klee. Translated by Marc Chénetier. Charenton: Editions Flohic, 1998.
Citizen Sidel. New York: The Mysterious Press, 1999.
Appelez moi Malaussène. Translated by Marc Chénetier. Paris: J'ai lu (Librio), 2000 [first published in *Le Monde*, 1996].
Hurricane Lady. New York: The Mysterious Press, 2001.
Under the Eye of God. New York: The Mysterious Press/Open Road, 2012.

Autobiographical writing

The Dark Lady from Belorusse: A Memoir. New York: St Martin's Press, 1997.
The Black Swan: A Memoir of the Bronx. New York: St Martin's Press, 2000.
Bronx Boy: A Memoir. New York: St Martin's Press, 2002.

Nonfiction

Metropolis: New York as Myth, Marketplace, and Magical Land. New York: Putnam, 1986.
Movieland: Hollywood and the Great American Dream Culture. New York: G.P. Putnam's Sons, 1989.
New York: Chronique d'une ville sauvage. Translated by Cécile Bloc-Rodot. Paris: Gallimard (Découvertes), 1994.
New York: Du Ventre de la Bête. Illustrations by François Boucq. Paris: Éditions DS, 1994.

Hemingway: Portrait de l'artiste en guerrier blessé. Translated by Cécile Bloc-Rodot. Paris: Gallimard (Découvertes), 1999.

Princess Hannah. Photos by Olivier Coulange. Translated by Jeanne Guyon. Arles: Actes Sud, 1999.

Sizzling Chops and Devilish Spins: Ping-Pong and the Art of Staying Alive. New York: Four Walls, Eight Windows, 2001.

Gangsters and Gold Diggers: Old New York, the Jazz Age, and the Birth of Broadway. New York: Four Walls, Eight Windows, 2003.

Savage Shorthand: The Life and Death of Isaac Babel. New York: Random House, 2005.

New York Sketchbook. Illustrations by Fabrice Moireau. New York: St. Martin's Press, 2005.

Raised by Wolves: The Turbulent Art and Times of Quentin Tarantino. New York: Thunder's Mouth Press, 2006.

Marilyn: The Last Goddess. New York: Abrams (Discoveries), 2008.

Joe DiMaggio: The Long Vigil. New Haven: Yale University Press, 2011.

Graphic novels

La Femme du magicien. With François Boucq. Paris: Casterman (Studio/ A Suivre), 1985 [*The Magician's Wife.* New York: Titan Books, 1988].

Margot in Badtown. With Massimiliano Frezzato. Grenoble: Glénat (Comics USA), 1986 [*Margot in Badtown.* New York: Heavy Metal Magazine: 1999].

Bouche du diable. With François Boucq. Paris: Casterman (Studio/ A Suivre), 1990 [*Billy Budd KGB.* New York: NBM, 1991].

Les Frères Adamov. With Jacques Loustal. Translated by Lili Sztajn. Paris: Casterman (Studio/ A Suivre), 1991.

Family Man. With Joe Staton. New York: Paradox Press, 1995.

Margot, Queen of the Night. With Massimiliano Frezzato. Grenoble: Glénat (Comics USA), 1995 [*Margot, Queen of the Night.* New York: Heavy Metal Magazine: 1999].

Le Croc du serpent. With José Muñoz. Paris: Casterman, 1997.

Une romance. With Jacques Loustal. Translated by Cécile Bloc-Rodot. Paris: Mille et une nuits, 1998.

Panna Maria. With José Muñoz. Translated by Frank Reichert. Paris: Casterman, 1999.

Madame Lambert. With Andreas Gefe. Translated by Jeanne Guyon. Paris: Editions du Masque/ Hachette, 1999.

White Sonya. With Jacques Loustal. Paris: Casterman, 2000.
Marilyn la Dingue. With Frédéric Rébéna. Translated by Lili Sztajn. Paris: Denoël Graphic, 2009.

Children and young adults fiction

Le Prince et Martin Moka. Illustrations by Jacques Loustal. Paris: Syros la Découverte (Souris Noir), 1988.
Back to Bataan. New York: Farrar, Straus & Giroux, 1991.
Bande à part. Illustrations by Jean-Claude Denis. Paris: Gallimard Jeunesse (Giboulées), 1995.
Otage à New York. Photos by Jean-Christian Bourcart. Translated by Marie-Pierre Bay. Paris: Gallimard (Folio junior), 1999.

Editions

The Single Voice: An Anthology of Contemporary Fiction. Editor. New York: Collier, 1969.
The Troubled Vision: An Anthology of Contemporary Short Novels and Passages. Editor. New York: Collier, 1970.
The New Mystery: The International Association of Crime Writers' Essential Crime Writing of the Late 20th Century. Editor. New York: Dutton, 1993.
The Crime Lover's Casebook. Editor. New York: Dutton, 1996.
Le Nouveau Noir Tome 1 et 2. Editor. Paris: Gallimard, 1997.
Inside the Hornet's Head. An Anthology of Jewish American Writing. Editor. New York: Thunder's Mouth Press, 2005.

Contents

Introduction xi

Chronology xvii

A Conversation with Jerome Charyn 3
Frederic Tuten / 1992

Raiding the City: An Interview with Jerome Charyn 26
Samuel Blumenfeld / 1992

Charyn, the Invention of Chaos 34
Serge Sanchez / 1993

An Interior Journey into the Belly of the Beast: *Metropolis* by Jerome
Charyn 38
Yann Lardeau / 1993

To Write Is to Die a Little: An Interview with Jerome Charyn 50
Sylvaine Pasquier / 1994

"Desperately Seeking for the Undersong": A Definition of Voice by Jerome
Charyn 57
LOLITA (Laboratoire Orléans-Tours de Littérature Américaine) / 1994

"Chanting in the Dark": An Interview with Jerome Charyn 70
Gilles Menegaldo / 1995

"Writing About": An Interview with Jerome Charyn 87
Marc Chénetier / 1995

From New York to the *Polar*: An Interview with Jerome Charyn 97
  Goulven Hamel / 1995

An Interview with Jerome Charyn 106
  David Seed / 1995

Jerome Charyn 110
  Frederic Tuten / 2004

"Pinocchio Is Still Out There": Listening to Jerome Charyn's Everlasting
Quest 118
  Sophie Vallas / 2009

Finding the Music: An Interview with Jerome Charyn on *The Secret Life of
Emily Dickinson* 147
  Richard Phelan and Sophie Vallas / 2011

Index 161

Introduction

In the United States Jerome Charyn is essentially known as a writers' writer, a writer whose audacity, ingenuity, and virtuosity are much praised by his peers but whose dense, protean work (as the bibliography contained in this volume makes obvious) often disconcerts both readers and critics. In France, though, where he has been living for longer and longer periods since the 1980s, Charyn has long been considered as a popular writer—ever since, in fact, the French met Isaac Sidel, Manfred Coen, and Marilyn the Wild in 1977 in the translation of *Blue Eyes*. In Paris, the legend has it that Charyn was the last author for whom editor Marcel Duhamel himself enthusiastically opened the doors of the famous Série Noire collection just before dying. From that moment on, Charyn's French readership has been expecting more volumes of Isaac's dark saga (now counting eleven volumes) while also welcoming his other literary experiences: the several graphic novels he cowrote with some of the best French and European artists, for instance, met with especially great success (he even won the highest distinction at the Angoulême festival for *The Magician's Wife*, cosigned by François Boucq), and the many books he published about New York as well as about American culture have established him as one of the best-known experts this side of the Atlantic.

It is therefore quite logical that most of the interviews contained in this volume should have been published in France, either in some of the best cultural magazines (*L'Express, Les Inrockuptibles,* or *Le Magazine littéraire*) or in academic journals (*GRAAT,* ENS Editions, or *E-rea*) when Charyn was interviewed by French researchers, including one of his historical translators, Marc Chénetier. As Charyn worked more and more in Paris, even publishing some of his books directly (and sometimes even exclusively) in their French translations, he started to punctuate his discourse with French words and expressions which have no exact equivalent in English and which testify to the new European landmarks he rapidly made his: the usual *roman noir* and *film noir*, of course, but also less transparent terms such as *polar* (a slang word for *roman noir* that Charyn confesses he especially likes[1]) or *bandes dessinées* (a genre which is somewhat in-between that of comic books and of graphic novels). Such terms, which also regularly pop up in the interviews given in the United States, have been kept in the transcriptions that were sometimes necessary to this volume.

The publication of Charyn's first *roman noir* in 1974 was obviously a turning point in his career: *Blue Eyes*, which he almost published under a pseudonym, suddenly brought him attention and fame after a few well-reviewed short stories and half a dozen experimental, postmodern, and unsuccessful novels. Surprised by the reception of the novel, Charyn started to read the classics of crime fiction which were still unknown to him and only then discovered the poisonous power of Dashiell Hammett, who remains his essential influence as far as *roman noir* is concerned: it is the way Hammett's detective "adds to the crime and is a criminal on the side of the law" (Menegaldo) that fascinates him, as well as Hammett's "very naked, very dry and cruel sentences" (Chénetier). But in the several interviews in which he is asked about his sudden turn towards crime fiction which made him so popular, he insists that his dark, *noir* novels are no different from his other novels, that he plays with genres and forms whatever the various labels people stick to his volumes. Writing essentially means "to sabotage the form, to push it to its limits, to play with it and yet make it moving at the same time," he asserts (LOLITA). France, known for its love for *polars*, is the only place in Charyn's eyes where readers actually see how he "twisted the whole genre around and stood it right on its head" (Seed). For him, everything is exclusively a question of language, and crime fiction is only a framework to "write explosive texts whose heroes and heroines happened to be police people" (Chénetier).

To Charyn, actually, the real turning point in his writing came less with *Blue Eyes* than with *Eisenhower, My Eisenhower*, three years before. "This is where I found my voice," Charyn keeps repeating throughout his interviews, adding that in his six previous novels, he had no music. His obsessive quest for the music of language, both in his own texts and in the works of other writers, would from that moment on be central to his work, and all of his interviews show him fighting to try and explain what he means by voice, style, rhythm, music, or undersong (see the LOLITA interview). The autobiographical background, which Charyn also generously discusses in his conversations, partly reveals the deep origins of this obsession. His parents—a Russian mother, a Polish father both fleeing misery and antisemitism—came to the United States as teenagers in the 1920s, and neither of them ever really managed to integrate into the New World society. The

Bronx ghetto where they ended up directly after going through Ellis Island was the barren landscape where they brought up their three sons without being able to prepare them for a faraway world which remained out of reach and undecipherable. "My background was a dead-end, a terrifying place; it had no language, no understanding of art," Charyn remembers (Vallas), picturing himself as a silent child: "I had no language as a child," he keeps repeating, as in the interview with Yann Lardeau in which he also explains that, as a child born to two immigrants who never succeeded in finding their place in the United States or even in mastering English, he still feels like an Ellis Islander, "neither European nor American. [. . .] Ellis Island is a kind of personal geography for me" (Lardeau). "I have no homeland, I only have two cities, New York and Paris," he continues like a masculine version of Josephine Baker (Blumenfeld). This deep conviction that he has no roots, no mother tongue, no family history to rely on turned Charyn into a "golem," a creature made of clay with no other choice but to invent itself.

Just like Pinocchio, the very first hero of his childhood to which he keeps returning and whose identity he borrowed in one of his most creative, autobiographical, and yet fantastic novels (*Pinocchio's Nose*, 1983), Charyn launched into mesmerizing adventures not in the Land of Toys but in the Land of Words. "I had to give birth to myself as a writer," he recently confessed (Vallas). In the course of this endless, experimental, joyful enterprise of autogenesis, Charyn has relentlessly explored the thin material of his family history (*Metropolis*, for instance, is an essay both on the history of New York City and on that of his immigrant family; *Panna Maria* is an evocation of the Polish paternal branch of his family tree) but has also never ceased to play with the very same incomplete material, redesigning his broken lineage and fantasizing his childhood in a Bronx which is long gone ("It feels very strange. I have no past I can go back to; I must either invent it or distort it" [Blumenfeld]) and which, thus re-created, is both highly realistic and entirely phantasmagorical. His recent autobiographical, or rather autofictional, trilogy (*The Dark Lady from Belorusse*, *The Black Swan*, and *Bronx Boy*) offers his readers a family romance in which Charyn's mother, the dark lady herself, literally radiates. "I wanted to give my mother a life that she should have had and never had," her son explains (Vallas), thus expanding on what he calls "mythopsychosis," a disease proper to writers who feel the urgent, irrepressible "need to narrativize their own lives" (LOLITA).

Charyn has thus progressively woven the legend of his family, and of course his interviews expand on the mythologization: his older brother Harvey, a homicide detective who opened for him the doors to the New York

City underworld of crime and who served as a model for Manfred Coen, Blue Eyes, the "sad killer angel" (Seed) who haunts Isaac's dreams as well as those of the readers of the saga, is often at the heart of the interviews. Simultaneously, Charyn both acknowledges his debt to him and unveils the way he turned him into a character, thus underlining the power of fiction. In his world indeed, police and criminals are the two sides of the same coin— both of them are gangsters on each side of the law, both of them evolve in a surrounding, never-ending chaos that they nourish, and both of them possess a form of romantic grace (flamboyant for the gangster, disenchanted for the cop). Charyn's gangsters are modeled on the great figures of crime in the 1940s and 1950s, the period of his childhood and of the climax of *film noir* which shaped his aesthetics: a time when the mobsters had their "own poetic language" and "an amazing body language"—"a real symphony of the body" (Blumenfeld). The writer's task, in his eyes, is also that of a gangster: "In my opinion language can kill," Charyn boldly asserts (Pasquier)—and he keeps quoting his mentors, Isaac Babel, for whom language was "an instrument of pain" (Seed) and Faulkner, who played with the irrationality of language to the very edge of chaos (Pasquier, Menegaldo). Language itself is "outside the law" (Seed), and the writer is a thief: " All writers, in some way, are criminals, because they take, they steal from the language—you know, the words are there for you to steal, you don't own them, you know, you have to steal them" (Menegaldo).

As the years and the interviews go by, Charyn more and more appears as a highwayman who steals words just like Jean Genet, whom he greatly admires. He is also a thief stealing voices, which is the very purpose of the writer as he explains to those readers baffled by his recent novel on Emily Dickinson—how could he thus appropriate her voice (see Phelan and Vallas)? Charyn's work is, indeed, beautifully interspersed with volumes devoted to other writers. If he is a writers' writer, as I said in the beginning, he also definitely is a writer who revels in *writing about* other writers, and his interviews testify to his love for those voices which have never ceased to whisper in his ears. *The Secret Life of Emily Dickinson* came after a short book devoted to Hemingway (*Hemingway: Portrait de l'artiste en guerrier blessé*) and a marvelous essay on Isaac Babel (*Savage Shorthand*), and before the novel *Jerzy Kosinsky*. In each case, Charyn shows his fascination for those writers who, in different ways, reinvented their lives and identities in their texts, multiplied masks and self-portraits sometimes to the point of dizziness and forgery. If those books are so difficult for traditional criticism to approach, it is essentially because they interweave the voices and lives of

Charyn and his models, intertwining their respective mythologies. "They're really about me," Charyn willingly confesses about those books that are the works of the "fan" he has always been, the child who remained eternally amazed and thankful when those voices started to invade his silent childhood.

Since the moment he discovered the power of language and the magic of literature, Charyn has never stopped straining his ears to discover how the writers he loves find "the music within the chaos" (Menegaldo)—something he endeavors to achieve in his own writing. "I always shy away from meaning," he explains to the LOLITA researchers. "I don't care what the meaning of the text is; I care what the music is because the meaning will come from that music." In his interviews, he keeps evoking Joyce, Hammett, Faulkner, Nabokov, Gass, Hawkes, and Melville, of course, who appears, more or less disguised, in every single one of his books. "One of the difficulties is: how do you communicate the mystery of a writer?" he asks at one point (Vallas). His whole work is a playful, colorful answer to this question.

This volume highlights Charyn's evolution in the course of his long career—from his early postmodern novels to his numerous graphic novels ("a universe in which all frontiers are abolished" [Blumenfeld]), his nonfictional essays on American cinema and culture, his unending exploration of New York by plunging into "the belly of the beast," his addictive, crazy crime fiction, his very personal historical novels, and finally to the very recent auto/biographical novels and essays. Whether in New York—which he knows by heart—or in Paris—which offers him a distance allowing him to dive even deeper into his memories as well as to question his language—in each one of these conversations Charyn obviously tries to convey his passion for a language that the silent, speech-impaired child he used to be had first to win after a long, brave fight, before finding his own, strange melody. "Yes, the inability to master language is often a language in itself," he whispered at the end of our long conversation in 2009, before confessing his fascination for those who are inarticulate. "Yes, really language is about no language. What I'm trying to do is make the unspeakable speak. That's the mission I have. To find a voice for those who have no voice." Just like somber Isaac, this once father-figure and then brother-figure who has accompanied him throughout his life, Charyn faces a challenge: Isaac's mission is to bring law and order into a world which is now resolutely lawless and chaotic, and although he perfectly knows that he is bound to fail, he remains nevertheless true to his mission in his own, unorthodox ways. Charyn's mission is to find a language in a yelling world, a music in a chaotic city, and his faith lies in one certainty: "words never really betrayed me. It's the only thing in my life that I felt—whatever lack of ability I have, whatever limitations I have—it's still to me—I don't know how to say—deeply *soothing* to write, whatever limits there may be in the writing [. . .]. I see texts as songs, as singers singing to soothe themselves: we're all sort of stuck in the same room trying to chant and chanting in the dark, it seems to me" (Menegaldo). The conversations gathered in this volume, as far as they are concerned, are luminous moments of singing and sharing.

Jerome Charyn was kind enough to support this project and to give me a long, moving interview on an grey, autumnal day in Paris, before coming down to the English Department of Aix-Marseille University to discuss *The Secret Life of Emily Dickinson* with researchers and students—both conversations are included in this book. He also helped a lot by giving his archives to the Fales Library, New York University, where I spent many a delightful day exploring the Jerome Charyn Papers. Finally, I am very grateful to all the editors and magazines who gave me permission to reprint the texts presented here, and to Walter Biggins and Craig Gill at the University of Mississippi, for making this volume possible.

SV

NOTE

1. In a brief interview which is not reprinted here, he says that he likes the "anti-establishment, subversive something" that the word *polar* suggests. Jean-Christophe Millois, "Entretien avec Jerome Charyn," *Prétexte* (1995, 18).

Chronology

1937	Jerome Charyn born on May 13 in the Bronx, New York, to Sam Charyn (a furrier), born in Poland, and Fannie Paley, born in Belorusse; raised in the Bronx, the second of three sons (Harvey and Marvin).
1955	Majors in painting at the High School of Music and Art in Manhattan. Receives scholarship for Columbia University where he studies history and comparative literature, with a focus on Russian literature.
1959	Graduates Phi Beta Kappa and *cum laude.*
1962–1964	Teaches English at the High School of Music and Art and at the High School of Performing Art in Manhattan.
1963	Charyn publishes his first short stories in *Commentary.*
1964	Charyn publishes his first novel, *Once upon a Droshky.*
1965	Marries Marlene Phillips, a writer. Charyn is a lecturer at City University of New York.
1966–1968	Charyn is assistant professor at Stanford where he participates in the "Voice Project" initiated by John Hawkes.
1968	The Charyns divorce. Charyn goes back to New York.
1968–1972	Charyn is assistant professor at City University of New York.
1970	Charyn creates and coedits the *Dutton Review* (only one issue was published).
1971	Charyn works for Otto Preminger. Publishes his seventh novel, *Eisenhower, My Eisenhower,* in which he now considers he finally found his voice.
1972–1978	Charyn is associate professor at City University of New York. He is the executive editor of *Fiction.*
1974	Charyn publishes *Blue Eyes,* the first volume of a long series of *romans noirs,* one of the heroes of which is modeled after his brother Harvey, a NYPD detective who is a specialist on the Mafia.
1978–1980	Charyn is visiting professor at City University of New York.

1981	Receives a National Endowment for the Arts grant and a National Endowment for the Arts Award for *The Catfish Man* (also selected by the *New York Times* as one of the best books of 1980).
1980–1986	Charyn is visiting professor at Princeton. He is a member of the Playwright/Directors Unit at the Actors Studio.
1981	Charyn receives the Rosenthal Foundation Award of the American Institute of Arts and Letters for *Darlin' Bill.*
1982	Charyn receives the John Simon Guggenheim Memorial Fellowship in Fiction.
1983	Wins a Guggenheim Fellowship for *Pinocchio's Nose.*
1985	Receives a National Endowment for the Arts grant.
1986	Charyn receives the highest distinction for the first graphic novel he wrote in collaboration with illustrator François Boucq, *La Femme du magicien,* at the Angoulême festival, France.
1992	Charyn's mother dies. Charyn starts living in Paris on a regular basis. The *Review of Contemporary Fiction* devotes a half-issue to his work.
1995	Charyn now spends half of his time in Paris. He works more and more with French editors and some of his books are published only in France.
1995–2009	Distinguished Professor of Film Studies at the American University of Paris.
2002	Charyn is made *Commandeur des Arts et des Lettres* by the French minister of culture.
2005	Finalist for the PEN/Faulkner Award for *The Green Lantern.*
2011	Finalist for Massachusetts Center for the Book Fiction Award for *The Secret Life of Emily Dickinson.*

Conversations with Jerome Charyn

A Conversation with Jerome Charyn

Frederic Tuten / 1992

From *Review of Contemporary Fiction*, 12.2 (Summer 1992): 96–114. Reprinted by permission of Frederic Tuten.

FT: Let's begin this way: you're a writer of how many novels?
JC: Twenty-two.

FT: But before your *bande dessinée, The Magician's Wife*, you had written about nineteen straight novels. How did the shift into the format of the *bande dessinée* come about?
JC: Well, I've always loved the idea of the graphic novel, but in the United States, where you have the Superman-Batman-superhero phenomenon in comic books, it seemed impossible to develop the form. In France, I saw that novels in illustrated form are very popular: we just don't have that here, with the exception of an illustrator like Windsor McCay and his one-page wonders. Since I was living in France much of the year, I made a real effort to see if I could do one, and it worked out. I was interviewed by a magazine called *A Suivre*, and they sent me the issue in which the interview appeared: there, I saw these wonderful illustrated stories. About two years later, I wrote the editor of the magazine and said I wanted to do one; he didn't speak a word of English, but we were able to communicate anyway, and I sent him the scenario of an abandoned novel.

FT: About characters in Saratoga?
JC: Yes. The ideas for *The Magician's Wife* came from a novel which just didn't work out. My main idea for the book was to have a lady werewolf who attacks men in Central Park—a comic theme against the backdrop of the 1970s. I never developed this into a novel, but in thinking about it for a *bande dessinée*, it was as if I were a kind of very weird movie director giving a signal and a word, and it comes back as an image. And I began to realize

how, maybe unconsciously, I had always had the desire to turn words into images. The illustrator for the *bande dessinée* religiously followed the first chapter of the scenario I had outlined, and I was delighted with it—maybe even more delighted than trying to reread one's own work; the illustrator gave a dimension to the words that they had never had before.

FT: So you sent them part of the unfinished novel, and they worked from there?

JC: I sent the outline of the story, and it was translated into French. The editor of the magazine liked it, and we found an illustrator who agreed to do it—that's how we began. But we soon ran into problems because the illustrator didn't speak English, and I wasn't in Paris that often. So I think, after the first part, he went off on a tangent, which I didn't like, though at least it wasn't totally disastrous.

FT: Did he alter the story line?

JC: Yes. For instance, I had thought of a detective who was a tough New York City cop. He changed him into a kind of Hercule Poirot who, in my opinion, didn't work well. So when the book was published in the United States, I changed the detective from a tough American cop into a comic French one, who is idiotic.

FT: So you discovered that doing a *bande dessinée* is like making a movie?

JC: Yes. You have all the problems of production, of working with a brilliant brute.

FT: The fortunate fact is that you have always had autonomy over your fiction. In truth, what you did was deliver up a script that goes through the same processes a movie script would go through. The book won . . . ?

JC: It won the prize at Angoulême given for the best *bande dessinée* published first in France, a kind of Academy Award for comics; there were hundreds of competitors.

FT: That's extraordinary. I'd like you to talk a little more about your fascination with doing this kind of work.

JC: Well, you have to remember that I started as an illustrator, because comic books were the only thing I read as a kid. Unfortunately, in the high school I went to, where I took art classes, comic books were frowned upon, so I had to do "serious painting." And I never continued studying this particular form. But I always loved it; I was insane about comic books because they didn't have to follow any kind of realistic mode. In comic books, you can go backward or forward. Look at George Herriman's *Krazy Kat*, for example, where the locale changes from panel to panel. And the humor. I think the possibilities for humor and romance and sexuality are infinite in a comic book; maybe they're infinite in the novel, but not quite in the same way, where the page has to follow a certain structure.

FT: Doesn't the form of the *bande dessinée* require a certain kind of precision and concision?

JC: I totally agree, but on the other hand because it is a comic book, it doesn't have the same demands on reality or logic that the novel usually follows, except for certain kinds of truly crazy books like *Tristram Shandy*. Usually, there's a realistic mode built into the novel which you can't get away from. There's a logic of sentence to paragraph to narrative which you don't have to follow in the *bande dessinée*.

FT: So this different form gave you a certain sense of your own liberty, and it excited you at a critical moment in your work.

JC: Well, I think that your life always takes a certain flow. When I went to Texas, suddenly Texas appeared in my work. When I worked at the Actors Studio, suddenly there was more dialogue in my novels, so I was writing plays in novel form. Actually, what I think I've been doing throughout my entire life is writing comic books in novel form. It doesn't seem to me that I was ever interested in realism, or logic, or traditional narrative. I think I've always been attracted by the surreal, the kind of fiction where anything can happen, where the form explodes and you have permutation after permutation like a chain reaction. That's the kind of fiction I've always wanted to write. So I think the move into the *bande dessinée* didn't come about because I was tired of writing fiction; it was a natural progression. Moving from novels into *bandes dessinées* and from *bandes dessinées* back into novels satisfied some deep need.

FT: And, of course, it's a logical extension of that idea to go from *bandes dessinées* into films? Can we talk a little about your film interests?

JC: Well, I'm very much interested in acting and in films which I want to do in France. Hollywood has made some incredible films, but I'm more interested in films where you have some kind of narrative outbreak, though this may be difficult or impossible to do in the way I would like to see it done.

FT: Give me an example of a model for this idea.

JC: Well, *Prizzi's Honor* seems to me a film that does this, where you have parody upon parody. And we could go back to Howard Hawks's classic—

FT: *The Big Sleep?*

JC: Yes, *The Big Sleep.* I think this is a wonderful film because it makes no sense whatsoever. There is no interior logic to it other than the movement from scene to scene. The same is true in *His Girl Friday.* Hawks was wonderful at creating his own weird logic in everything he did. You find the same thing in *Gunga Din,* George Stevens's film, and of course *Duck Soup* is the archetype for the kind of film where nothing makes sense, and yet which has its own internal order. That's the sort of work in film I would like to do.

FT: But in your fiction, there is a kind of realism; you wouldn't call your fiction phantasmagorical?

JC: No.

FT: So the *bande dessinée* and film would allow you a kind of license, though I think your fiction combines realism, a concern for contemporary life, and what you're talking about as occurring in films and comic books. For example, in *Pinocchio's Nose*—

JC: —you have permutation within permutation. And I became "Pinocchio" in *Pinocchio's Nose*, so that was as far as I could go. But that book was so poorly received in the United States, so misunderstood, that I didn't know what to do after that. *War Cries over Avenue C* has the same kind of craziness, but again, the reception was so bizarre that I became incredibly discouraged. I didn't have the energy or courage to just say "fuck it" and do what I wanted to do; I had this sense of a marketplace and it frightened me, because I hate marketplaces. But I think in these two books, and in my novel about baseball, *The Seventh Babe,* and maybe in *The Catfish Man,* which starts out traditionally enough but then moves into a fantasy world . . . there was a kind of lyric joy for me in writing those novels, but the way in which they were received killed some of the joy, so I had to snake in a different direction.

FT: It seems ironic that you would have to go to France to find a form that amused and haunted you, and an audience who would be receptive to it. I think the narrative drive that you're talking about exists in *The Magician's Wife,* and it's the sort of thing you would find in great films, where you are swept away by the first image to the last. But I also think this occurs in the novels you mentioned. Has *The Magician's Wife* been a popular success?

JC: Yes, very successful and very popular, like many of the *bandes dessinées*; it's been published all over the world.

FT: Including the United States?

JC: Including the United States, where again, it had nowhere near the reception it had in Europe. I think it's because the graphic novel is not a form that is understood in this country. First of all, the European *bande dessinée* is very, very sexy. It's rooted in the kind of sexuality which would be tolerated in a novel but not in image form.

FT: One of the things I think we feel is that what we call comic books are light entertainment for children or idiots who can't read a text. I'd like to get back to film for a moment: do you have any aspirations to make a film?

JC: Well, not as a director, but I have written screenplays. I'm more interested in writing for the theater: I've written a play about King George III and I'm hoping it might be put on in France. But again, I find the screenplay a bastard form, a model for the director to play with. So what I would like to do is both write and act in films. I don't have the technical facility to be a director, and I don't have the interest in carefully editing images even though I love them. But the problem is that a screenwriter's work is dismissed once it gets into the director's hands, and that's not the kind of brutality that I would like to see with my own work. The screenwriter never owns his work; it's always bought out from under him. That's not entirely true with the graphic novel: I feel it's mine even though the illustrator's work is probably more important than that of the person who does the narrative or the scenario. I have a tremendous amount of pleasure in deciding what might go into each panel, maybe something like Hitchcock, who outlined each of his shots. Of course, he was the director and knew what he was going to do, and I'm not the director of the comic book. But in a way, I am, because when you work with the right kind of illustrator, it's a delight to see your words transcribed into images. Now, I'm working with an illustrator, Loustal, on a *bande dessinée* called *The Boys of Sheriff Street*, which is about two gangsters in New York in the thirties who are twins, one of whom has a slight hunchback. Loustal is wonderful to work with: he is probably the foremost artist in the form, and each panel is a work of art, extraordinarily beautiful.

FT: What other things has he done?

JC: There's *Barney and the Blue Note*, about a jazz musician, which was very successful in France and has also been published here.

FT: Are you working on a novel now?
JC: Yes, I'm working on another book, and *The Good Policeman* just came out [published in July 1990 by The Mysterious Press]; it's the fifth volume about a detective, Isaac Sidel. To go back to an earlier subject, I do feel that my novels are becoming much simpler in format. They're not anywhere as complicated as, let's say, *Pinocchio's Nose*, and they don't have that quality of the fantastic. Maybe, in a sense, they're closer to being graphic novels without the graphics.

FT: There are some constants in your fiction, even though it has changed over the years. One of my favorites is the character of the idiot in your fiction, which appears in very early published work.
JC: Yes, in a novel called *Once upon a Droshky*, about an old Yiddish actor on the Lower East Side, published in 1964.

FT: How old were you then?
JC: Twenty-six, though there's a story about a girl, "Faigele the Idiotke," which I published in *Commentary* a year earlier.

FT: So the theme of the idiot exists in your fiction from the earliest days, or more precisely the idea of the odd, the infantile, the theme of the helpless child?
JC: Yes. It's like a video of myself. I often feel like an imbecile in that I'm incompetent in everything I do, maybe even in the writing. But the only thing that doesn't frighten me is writing. I feel a tremendous sense of joy and power in doing the work, and I'm never frightened at all to do a book. But I have a fear of going places and of letting people down in some way, whether it's a class or a friend—it's a kind of disease of incompetence. But it doesn't touch me when I write. That same sense of joy and power maybe comes only when you're in love and making love to a woman, but that is very, very rare. The lyricism is what does it: the only time it didn't work was when I was in California and very unhappy. So I was the imbecile for three and a half years—the same thing happened once when I was in Texas—and I was completely frozen, very frightened. My natural inclination is to be a hermit, to sit at home and do my work, which is a horrible kind of life. But it seems to me it's the only way I can write, as a phantom moving from one culture into

another culture. To go back to the idea of the idiot: I've always felt incredible sympathy for the figure of the idiot because he's a kind of genius. You think of people like Einstein, misfits who just happened to have a particular flash of genius. Those are the people for whom I feel the most sympathy, and all of my characters—young, old, male, female—are like that, like perverse children, like the character in "The Man Who Grew Younger," a story about a Yiddish poet who writes a story about a man who grows younger. It's an obsession that runs through all of my work.

FT: So there's a sense that the characters you're drawn toward are failures, but also "saint" figures, in that they don't compete in the real world.
JC: Sometimes they do. For example Isaac, in his own way, is very successful. He starts in *Blue Eyes* as a deputy chief inspector, and by the time of *Secret Isaac*, he's the police commissioner of New York. And how does he get success? By killing people. At the other end of the spectrum is the idiot hit man of *Paradise Man*.

FT: I found it remarkable that you made a hit man the protagonist of *Paradise Man*; he commits a crime, and there is no judgment made about it. Could you say more about this?
JC: Well, I think of the main character [Manfred Coen] in *Blue Eyes*; the reader must be shocked when "Blue Eyes" dies. I think the reader assumes that Paradise Man is going to die from the first page, and he doesn't. In the sequel, *Elsinore*, he goes from being a hit man to someone who tries to avoid killing people, even though it seems as if he's going to have to kill everyone in order to avoid getting killed.

FT: You've already mentioned the film about a hit man in love, *Prizzi's Honor*.
JC: Yes. I know other people have reservations about the film, but I think it's one of Huston's best works—it has a playfulness that had been absent from his films for some time. In a sense, it's a film about a wolfman—Jack Nicholson even looks like a wolfman—but it's also a film about pure, absolute play. I was delighted it was a success, because it is almost too intelligent to be successful.

FT: You don't feel that either you or Huston make judgments about protagonists who are killers?
JC: I think you're made to feel sympathetic; you don't want them to be hurt.

I wouldn't say this of *Prizzi's Honor*, but every murder Holden commits [in *Paradise Man*] seems almost to come out of a desire not to hurt someone else, and not to be hurt himself. He's very much in tune with American culture, which is one great killing field.

FT: American culture?
JC: Well, American nonculture, since we don't really have a culture. We have a history of amnesia, but not a real culture.

FT: There's a lot of violence in your work; is that America, for you?
JC: There's a lot of violence in the American landscape. I grew up, as you did, in an environment filled with violence. It was everywhere; you couldn't avoid it.

FT: But we didn't grow up in a place, in the Bronx, where there were hit men.
JC: No, but in my neighborhood, the great hero was always the local tough who never survived his own childhood. Every kind of "total gangster" that I knew as a kid never reached the age of eighteen. And they were sad, tragic—it was like Sophocles in the Bronx! This was something I was really drawn to, and I always fantasized myself in this environment as being outside the law. But this was the romantic image of a ten-year-old imbecile. I'd never really read books when I was a kid.

FT: How old were you when you started to read books?
JC: Well, I read the things I had to in public school, but outside of that, I only read comic books until the age of seventeen, when I read *The Sun Also Rises*, which I thought was incredible. Other than Hemingway, and reading *The Sound and the Fury* and *One Hundred Years of Solitude*, there's nothing, I swear, beyond the age of ten that has really influenced my work. Everything in the last twenty-five years of my work was already formulated when I was ten years old. That may seem a sad and pathetic thing to say, and it may be regressive to have moved backward. But I think I was defined by two things: World War II and the movies. Nothing ever touched me as much as films did, and still do now. I've never left in the middle of a film, except when I went to see *Sea of Love*—the projector broke down in the middle of the film, and I was *destroyed*. Not because it was a great film, but because I didn't have the luxury of coming out of the movie and feeling that complete bliss of termination. The film is over, you feel great. You go to the movies, into this landscape—the idiot gets out of his own head, and then returns to the

dark. For example, and I'm not lying to you, I've seen *Prizzi's Honor* at least thirty-five times, and each time I see it, I enjoy it more; but what can I say, I'm an imbecile!

FT: What about growing up during the war, about your family?
JC: I come from a family that I find very bizarre. I've been angry at my mother for a long, long time, and it's only recently that I've gotten rid of this anger. I was never really able to break out of my family and form my own family. I was married once, but I have no children; I was never able to leave my family, even though, in a literal sense, I left when I was twenty-four; but I never made a complete break. In some way, all of my work involves family ties, family relationships.

FT: It's true; in the Isaac novels I see all of those rich, wonderful characters longing for an extended family, one that crosses all national boundaries, even time and space. The bloodlines go so deep that once you're in those families you know you're protected for life.
JC: Right.

FT: Even if you're the idiot.
JC: Exactly.

FT: So, in a sense, you're the eternal child?
JC: Yes. I feel incompetent, childlike, in every way outside of the writing. I mean, even coming back from Paris to New York, I had to orchestrate an entire scenario in terms of getting the ticket, getting someone to drive me to the airport, having someone hold my hand when I went to the ticket counter to make sure that the ticket was in my name. Because, to me, the world seems so perversely magical that I never believe anything is going to turn out right. I'm always terrorized.

FT: Do you think this has anything to do with being Jewish, and raised by people who were immigrants in America?
JC: How so?

FT: People who are always foreigners in this culture, who don't understand the rules of the game. And, basically, the relationship of the immigrant to the culture is that of the child to the parent who is distant and powerful—
JC: And perverse?

FT: —and perverse. And you can't be quite sure that today's pat on your back won't be tomorrow's club on your head.

JC: Exactly. And you may escape it for a little while, but the hangman is always going to be there. If he's not around this corner, he's around the next corner. My worst suspicions are always confirmed in the world. Other people wouldn't mind if they arrived at the airport five minutes before the plane takes off because they always have the trust that somehow the plane will wait for them; or, what is the real tragedy if I missed my plane—I can always get another one. But somehow it seems that the journey from Paris to New York is incredibly immense—it seems like you're traveling to outer space, and that you'll never get back. Other than the deep-rooted fear that there will be an air crash, there's always the suspicion that you'll be caught somewhere, and that the plane will never land. There are these immense journeys.

FT: So, in your novels, you always have to have a competent character to guide the idiot around.

JC: Yes.

FT: Getting back to your family: you have two brothers, and one is a police detective. Does he—that character in your novels—represent the good side of the world, or the character who escapes routine, who enters the world of fluidity and excitement? How has your brother influenced your work?

JC: Well, of course, the detective books that I have written are, in part, based on his own life and make use of his expertise. What I find interesting about my brother is the combination of sadness and intelligence I think most homicide detectives have, having seen the absolute brutality of life. And yet, in his own way, he's also an imbecile. He's also afraid of flying, but at least I was able to get on a plane: he refused to fly, I think, until he was forty-five years old. I would swear he still doesn't have a checkbook, though I may be wrong. His competency is being out on the streets; my competency is in writing books, but I don't think they're that much different from each other. I think we share a similar intelligence, and a similar sadness. He's one of the few people that I love and trust, because we come out of the same labyrinth, the same emptiness.

FT: Could you say a little more about that—where you came from?

JC: I couldn't make any connections. I never went into Manhattan until I was fourteen. I think the whole Bronx was a world which had no context, no center of gravity. The borough itself makes no sense. It's a kind of bed-room community that goes nowhere, comes from nowhere, and is always a path toward someplace else. People who are born in the Bronx don't stay there unless they're deeply troubled—it's always a route to somewhere else. I always fantasize that I'd grown up on the Lower East Side, where there are real neighborhoods, contexts. But the Bronx is just endless streets and indistinct neighborhoods. Growing up there, I felt like I had fallen to the earth and landed somewhere, and just suddenly started walking away from where I fell.

FT: But there were neighborhoods in the Bronx when we were growing up: the Jewish neighborhood, where you were raised; the Italian neighborhood around Arthur Avenue.
JC: Yes, there were, but these were just pockets within a crazy island. The Italians always created a community, and the most extraordinary areas of New York are still the Italian neighborhoods, because Italians don't have this desire to move from place to place.

FT: What about the Jewish neighborhood you grew up in?
JC: It was a neighborhood of Jewish louts. I was not only the first person in my family to go to college; I was the first one in the whole *community* to go to college. And this is not the traditional image we have of Jews.

FT: What kind of Jews were they?
JC: These were Jewish gangsters! These were people who had no education, and no interest in education. The only book in my house was the first vol-ume of *The Wonderland of Knowledge*, which went from AA to BA. So I knew the history of the world according to A. I memorized the entire book, so you ask me anything starting with the letter A, and like an idiot savant, I would give it back to you. But that's it; it ended at that particular point. I think that was indicative of the whole Bronx. The Jews I grew up with were the toughest kids in the neighborhood; therefore it was perfectly logical that my brother became a policeman, because it was a legalized way of beating people up! I don't mean to say that this was his character, but it was the Wild West. It was absolutely primitive, so what could you do? I ended up writing comic books: the high point of culture for me as a child was some-thing called "Classic Comics," which were comic books that took novels like *Lorna Doone* and turned them into an illustrated history. And even they, out of some kind of desperation, changed the term "comic book" to "Classic

Comics"—later it became "Classics Illustrated"—in order to get outside of the genre. I remember the greatest blow of my childhood: I'd always wait religiously for the next issue of "Classic Comics"—I think they came out once a month or once every other month. And then when it became "Classics Illustrated" it was a tremendous descent into nowhere, because suddenly it was terribly pretentious—even the drawings changed. So I couldn't even read *Lorna Doone* and *Ivanhoe* in peace.

FT: How did you draw on your brother's experiences in writing your detective novels?

JC: I ran around with him; I drew on his lingo; I listened to his stories. And I was tremendously moved by the cop stories, because they have lives that, in a profound way, are very grim. Many of them are alcoholic, divorced, very unhappy people. My brother was the protective guy who turned on me at a certain point; but I don't think I would have been able to survive without him, because there was such hostility between my father and myself that only a moral buffer—my brother—could protect me. My father had a curious combination of rage and impotence, and I can remember one of the strangest experiences of my life was when my father got angry at my brother—I mean, it was a tremendous rage. He threw a broom at my brother which hit him right in the eye. It was just horrible. I don't know how my older brother was able to contain his rage, because he was very strong; he was a weightlifter and eighteen years old. He could have demolished my father, and somehow, he didn't. I've never understood that: it was such a violent gesture, and his whole eye was bruised—he could have *lost* his eye. And he didn't do anything. I was amazed, really dumbfounded; I don't think I would have been able to contain myself.

FT: I thought you lifted weights, too.

JC: I did. I was the youngest weightlifter in the *Guinness Book of Records*. I began very early, when I was a skinny, wretched kid. And at the age of twelve I had enormous muscles. I thought it was tremendously boring and dropped it by the time I was fourteen. But for a while, I was this muscle-bound geek, the Li'l Abner of the Bronx! The first magazines I read were about bodybuilders—Steve Reeves, Mr. America—these were my heroes other than the murderers.

FT: Let's skip to the present: what is the current book you're working on?

JC: I've recently finished the sequel to *Paradise Man*, called *Elsinore,* and I'm working on a screenplay for *Paradise Man*. It seems strange to work on the screenplay of one's own novel because you're into the bones of the book; it's like re-haunting one's own work.

FT: You've also written a book on film [*Movieland*]. Can we talk more about your involvement with film?

JC: I've done several filmscripts, but the problem is that I'm not particularly interested in commercial film and the schematic impositions that go with Hollywood. So I've only had bad experiences in working with producers who hire you because they say they love your work, and then, when you try to be faithful to what they seem to think they want, it turns into a disaster. I suppose it's just simple narcissism: they hope that you'll give them back whatever it is deep inside them that they can't reach themselves. And of course, there's no way you can do that, so what they want is a phantom version of their own insanities. I've had nothing but the greatest displeasure working in film, and it seems to me it's never even worth the money because, first of all, you don't own the material, and second, it's almost never done. So the screenplay I'm working on now is noncommercial, for a low-budget film. I wanted to work on it simply because I didn't want anyone else to take the text and oversimplify it.

FT: Didn't you once work for Otto Preminger? Would you talk about that episode for a moment?

JC: I was in my middle or late thirties, and he had fallen so low that no one would work for him. He hired me—you can see what despair he was in, because I had no film credits whatsoever. He didn't know who I was, he had never read a word I'd written, but he hired me immediately because he was so desperate. I found him to be a wonderful, enchanting man. He had married, perhaps for the third time, and had a son and daughter, twins about twelve years old. And I was absolutely amazed to see what a wonderful father he was. He was totally delighted with these kids, and at the same time, he was the image of Otto Preminger the ogre, the man who fired Lana Turner and who had destroyed people's careers. But I loved him because, first of all, I had never considered myself a screenwriter, so when he called me an imbecile and told me I didn't know how to write and that I ought to be shot, I laughed! And he loved it. He couldn't get to me. He'd say that my work wasn't worth ten cents, and I would laugh.

FT: You weren't hurt or chagrined?

JC: I didn't give a shit! I never considered myself a screenwriter, and here I was, earning an *unthinkable* amount of money—$1500 a week, much more than I could have earned elsewhere. He demanded that I work six days a week, but of course I did *nothing*: I would piddle over two pages.

FT: What was the project?
JC: CBS had him on line to do a television project on the Supreme Court, focusing on Justice Hugo Black. And I reworked a script that had been revised several times already and was dreadful. I think I made it a little better, but he couldn't get a yes even from CBS, he had fallen so low. It was sad, because he was a multimillionaire with his own film company, but he couldn't get anyone to buy his work. I was just marking time. I wanted to get out of the arrangement, so I told him one day, "Otto, look, I'll work for you one day for free if you'll let me out of this." He was so taken aback, he couldn't understand what I was talking about, but he saw that he was going to get one free day. So I worked the free day, which meant I worked for ten minutes on two pages, fell asleep, and left. He was completely shattered, not because anything had happened, but because having a writer gave him the sense that something was in process. He had an enormous office, like Il Duce, with an anteroom next to it, so I was at his beck and call—that is, he could come in through the rear door and spy on me anytime he wanted. It was a little like *1984*. I never thought he was a great director, though I loved *Laura*. I really loved him as an actor in *Stalag 17*, you know, as the eternal Prussian Nazi, like Eric von Stroheim.

FT: Were any of the screenplays you wrote close to being realized as films?
JC: I worked with Arthur Penn, and with Richard Harris. But with screenplays, they lie asleep for ten years, and then one day, who knows—maybe all of this stuff will be made, one never knows.

FT: Do you think that some of the constructions of your books have been based on cinematographic models?
JC: Absolutely. If you look at *Paradise Man*, it's not only film, it's theater. For me, films have always been a primal influence; I've always thought about the one sentence that will give you a complete picture. But I think it goes back further than that, once again, to comic books. I couldn't stand *not* to read comic books. I had a collection of over a thousand comics: I read them over and over again; I can't describe to you what they mean as the embodiment of an *absolute* sense of play. In film, even the craziest ones—with the possible exception of the Marx Brothers movies—there is a literal sense of

reality that you have to adhere to. And this is never true in comic books. There is always that total, irrevocable sense of play where nothing is certain on the page. This is what I rediscovered when I saw comics in Europe in the eighties, and the wonderful things that the European illustrators were doing. That's when I began writing scenarios.

FT: So, with the graphic novel, unlike film, it's as if you own the book, and in a way, working with an artist doing the drawings is really about *directing* in a certain sense.

JC: Absolutely. In the case of the artist I'm working with now, Loustal, he shows me the pages he's made from my script and I don't think of it as mine or his; it really doesn't matter: from a word you get a magic image.

FT: With comic books, we're back to childhood again. *Red Ryder* and *Prince Valiant* and cap pistols.

JC: Yes, that magical world, though it seems to me that I was never happy as a kid, not for five minutes. And yet, adulthood seems like some horrible, strange, endless fall towards death, but without a release. The kind of wonder or fascination that you had as a kid, the leaps of imagination, not planning the future—it's the magical possibilities that were out there. Let's say in the comic book or the cap pistol: a kind of release. I remember getting a whistling ring, the gold special—I'd been waiting for weeks and suddenly this package arrived, and I was delirious. I opened it up and there was this wonderful ring, and I remember my brother had one of those guns that projected images on the wall. I must have been six years old, or maybe even younger, but I thought it was one of the most extraordinary things in the world, because he projected images on the wall, and the images told a story. I think that's one of the reasons that I write: when we're kids, we need stories, the line of history, the continuity of the tale; I think that need probably never leaves us.

FT: Is there a connection between the violence you remember in your childhood, and the sense of release or magic?

JC: I'm not sure. All I know is that my childhood seemed filled with outlaws. One of the most extraordinary events of my childhood was seeing two Italian twins—outlaw brothers—having a fight. It was like *The Mark of Zorro*: they fought up and down an entire street for three hours, an endless, irrevocable, medieval battle between two outlaws. And then, at the end of the fight, they were as loving as they had been hateful during the fight.

FT: Where was this?

JC: Back again in my neighborhood in the Bronx. It was, as Coppola would say in *Apocalypse Now*, the asshole of the world. No one ever went there, and if you go there now, either the streets are in ruins or they don't exist or they've been changed into something unrecognizable. The fight happened on Seabury Place, right near Charlotte Street, but everything there has been turned into ranch houses; it's now a field of ranch houses. In other words, the whole past that I had as a kid is in ruins; it no longer exists. It's strange, but each time I go back there and see the streets so changed, I have a tremendous feeling of power—not fright, not regret. I have a magical feeling of revoking the past, even though the past has completely disappeared. I think of the past as horrible, unpleasurable, except for the movies and walking. I loved to walk those streets. For me, when I walk, I have no sense of time.

FT: Do you still walk, in New York and Paris?

JC: I walk everywhere.

FT: I think all of the women in your books are outlaws; they have a weird kind of autonomy that I don't quite understand. They're so magnetic and compelling; they're powerful women.

JC: Well, they're not women who are subject to men. They're not "good wives"; they're people who are completely and irrevocably independent.

FT: Which characters would you think of in this regard?

JC: The women in *Paradise Man* and *Marilyn the Wild*, or the women in *Panna Maria*. Even if they are happily married they're never with their husbands. The essential situation is that the family has broken down. To go back to my own family, I've never written about my mother, but in a masked way, maybe some of the women in the novels are, not reflections of, but dialogues with my mother.

FT: Although she's the perfect example of the mother who stays home?

JC: Yes, she's the mother who stayed home; on the other hand, she had a peculiar kind of independence. I don't know how to describe it: there was a creature locked within her, a kind of Marilyn the Wild who never came out. The older I get, the more it seems that I'm right back where I started with my family: so, literally, I've gone nowhere; it's been a trek to nowhere. Which is OK, as long as you understand it and don't grieve for it. I was married once, but I can't seem to have a day-by-day existence with a woman; it makes me crazy. I don't know why, but I can't breathe.

FT: The characters in your novels seem to create relationships based on not having relationships.

JC: Yes, they're nomads, strange creatures in an eternal desert. When I started coming to Europe, I thought I was a European rather than an American; now, I think I'm not even a European, but a desert creature. I don't know where I came from, but it must have been from some landscape or atmosphere that is so overpowering there's nothing else to do. When I read Paul Bowles's *Sheltering Sky*, I thought it was an extraordinary book, because he deals with this very thing: the enigma of identity; whatever it is that keeps us going, is something we're profoundly frightened of.

FT: Maybe that explains my sense that your fiction is filled with rich, complex, moving characters, that your imagination is one of the richest in American writing today. No one I know has the same range, or variety, or angle of vision, the varieties of vision, the literal sense of the streets and the world behind the buildings.

JC: Again it goes back to childhood: as a kid I was always playing, always going behind the couch and pretending, and it's never left me. Sometimes, I feel exhausted as a writer, and I feel I can't do the long books that I would have been able to do at one time, but so what? One of the things that is always delightful is when you invent a character on the page; that's why I create so many characters, an endless sea of characters, rather than just sticking with two or three and analyzing them into infinity. I'll have forty characters within the same landscape. I'm a little bit unhappy about a book like *Panna Maria* which, perhaps, is *too* rich, where the fantasy level of the imagination has gone too far, like a strange flower that strangles itself. But in that novel, I really wanted to tell the story of immigrant Americans. I didn't want to write about a Jewish family, which would have been logical and autobiographical. I had to do it in a perverse way, so I focused on Poles, whom I hated, even though my father is Polish; but you have to remember that the Poles were terribly anti-Semitic. I created a Polish family, a tribe of prostitutes, and used them to make an image of the New World. When the book came out, I started getting hate letters from Polish generals, saying, "Why didn't you write about the Jews?" That's to assume that I could only write about Jews, and that I picked Poles because I was anti-Polish, that I was writing another Polish joke. But I picked Poles because I thought of them as a wonderful emblem of America—brutal, wild, unassimilated folk. The name of the main character in the book is Stefan Wilde—in a way, my own Stephen Dedalus. His job is to go to Ellis Island and take all of the unmarried women who come in, pretend to be their husband, and then bring them to the whorehouse. But I couldn't stick with that one image; the book is full of mutant images that suddenly change the landscape. There was nothing I could do about it. Then there is a book like *War Cries over Avenue C* that, literally, doesn't make sense unless you think of it in terms of music.

FT: Right.

JC: Or if you think of it in terms of *Krazy Kat*, where the panels keep changing, why do you need continuity? Why do you need linear perspective? It means nothing. So it always saddens me when I see the reception to my novels because critics are always making realistic demands on works that aren't meant to be realistic. I mean, as if I didn't know what to do if I wanted to write a realistic novel. The fact is, I'm not dealing with a realistic universe and the expectations or distrust that a reader who wants realism might have. One of the reasons I've turned toward writing plays and doing the *bandes dessinées* is that I feel a profound *sadness* about the novel. Not that I will abandon the form, but that I have no expectations whatsoever.

FT: I wanted you to talk a little about some of your early novels, like *Eisenhower, My Eisenhower*, because we've only talked about the later books. I just looked at it again today, and I see that you use a quote from Ginsberg.

JC: Yes. "If we're alive, then who is dead?" It's a perfect quote. I think *Eisenhower, My Eisenhower* is my first book, really. The ones before were exercises, but that's the book where I found my voice. It's probably a bit self-indulgent and overdone.

FT: But it has a beat, an energy. Is it presumptuous to say that the prose has a kind of Beat Generation energy to it?

JC: Well, it was written after I'd been in California, from 1965 to 1968.

FT: What were you doing there?

JC: I was teaching at Stanford, and I was really involved in the antiwar movement; it was during the worst time in the Vietnam War period, and it was all very sad. I was married at the time, but very unhappily married. I came back to New York thinking that I wouldn't stay because I was supposed to go and teach at Berkeley, but for some reason, I didn't. When I first got back, I hated the city. I couldn't stand the noise, and I would go into the subway and be frightened. Then suddenly, I began to love it again. I fell into the rhythm and wrote this very crazy book which is about gypsies with tails who are involved in an urban revolution. I really believed that something was going on in the sixties, that we were pushing the leviathan aside. I believed it foolishly, and that's why I wrote the book. I felt that it was the first work of fiction where I found my voice. I had mimicked other voices in other books, but this was mine. And from that point on, I felt I had become a writer. It didn't matter to me, at that point, how the novel would be received, even though I knew it was going to be bad.

FT: Why did you think that?
JC: Because the other books were so stupidly received, so in a way, I had given up.

FT: Which books do you mean?
JC: There was a collection of short stories, there was *Going to Jerusalem*, about a fanatical chess player, there was *American Scrapbook*, which was about the Japanese American internment camps. There was *Once upon a Droshky*, which was my first novel. But *Eisenhower* was the novel where I'd really discovered how to write. In a way, I had to be away from New York and then come back; I think it was the celebration of being back in New York after the experience of the California years that allowed me to write *Eisenhower, My Eisenhower*.

FT: Which writers have influenced you? I keep thinking that I see in your work the same passionate, driving energy, the ferocity of language, or trying to break through the skin of the real world, that you find in Melville, in *Mardi* or *Moby-Dick*.
JC: Yes, I love Melville. Faulkner and Nabokov are the two writers whom I absolutely adore. And I have a grudging admiration for Henry James and for the power that he has, though I can't love him because he's always under such absolute control. Except for a few moments when his work breaks into a dream for me, as it does in "The Beast in the Jungle." And with Nabokov it's a very short period, from *Lolita* to *Pale Fire*. It was during the last phase of his being in America, it seems to me, that it all came together for him. *Lolita* was the culmination of his attempt to trap the English language, to really catch the butterfly. I think he really caught the butterfly perfectly in *Lolita*.

FT: Speaking of Nabokov, what about your parody, *The Tar Baby*?
JC: *The Tar Baby* is in the form of a literary magazine. It's a special issue devoted to this bizarre character who is a Wittgenstein fanatic, self-taught, who teaches at a junior college.

FT: Is the novel still in print?

JC: No, it's out of print, but at least it was published in the first place. After I wrote *The Tar Baby*, I wrote a book about the Bronx called *A Child's History of the Bronx* which no one would publish.

FT: I remember seeing part of it in *Statements*, the Fiction Collective's anthology. It was one of the most beautifully written pieces of writing I've ever read. What came next?

JC: I wrote *Blue Eyes*, because I felt I was in some kind of hole.

FT: *Blue Eyes* was a big switch for you, because it's your first police book.

JC: Yes, and it came out of a kind of desperation. The fiction I had been writing up to that point . . . maybe I should have tried a publisher like New Directions, but the kind of work I was doing, where I wanted to carry things to the ends of rationality, didn't seem to have any advocates or fans. So I switched to the detective fictions, these police novels which bear no relation to any other police novels.

FT: How so?

JC: Well, they're just as problematic as the earlier novels; they have nothing to do with police procedures; they're not mysteries.

FT: They're about men living at the edge who happen to be policemen.

JC: Exactly, and the nature of the novels seems to make them more acceptable to readers. The characters live in a world where there are no connecting links, because they are policemen and, therefore, they don't need any connections. After *Blue Eyes*, I wrote another novel called *King Jude*, about a Nazi king in a very little country near Andorra which I named "Whalebone." The novel had no center, no focus in any traditional sense, and I didn't even send it around. Then, because I had killed off "Blue Eyes," Manfred Coen, I became interested in that character and did a "prequel" in *Marilyn the Wild*. Then, *The Education of Patrick Silver* and *Secret Isaac* followed in the series, but in between, I wrote a novel about Roosevelt called *The Franklin Scare* which, again, had no reception whatsoever. At that point, I felt I had gone about as far as I could go with those characters, and now, twelve-fifteen years later, I've gone back to the Isaac character in *The Good Policeman*.

FT: How do you feel about contemporary writing?

JC: I think most of it is journalism at best. Most of it has no sense of any aesthetic form and no sense of the beauty of words; play is gone. But one keeps on working; we were always amnesiacs, but now it's amnesia squared.

FT: But obviously there's an interested and intelligent readership for you. In a way, what more could we ask for than to get our books published, though there's a certain sense of injustice.

JC: I don't think it's injustice; one never expects to have a just world. You have to think of your books in relation to everything that surrounds them. I find the whole mechanism of book publishing and book reviewing very disturbing. There's very little place for the outlaw or maverick writer, but you still have to keep writing.

FT: Who do you consider outlaw writers today? Burroughs?

JC: Yes, some Burroughs; some of your work. Some of the early William Gass, Stanley Elkin, the very early Grace Paley. And of course there are many others, but it seems to me that the whole idea of language and the excitement of language is no longer there. You can't pick up a page as you could, let's say twenty-five years ago, and say "Ah! This is something I really want to read!" I don't find it anywhere.

FT: You've been teaching for many years, in California, at Princeton, and CCNY. What is your relationship to students in the workshops? What does it give you? What does it give them? What hopes do you see there?

JC: When the writing is serious, or when you see someone who really wants to be a writer, I think you can be very helpful. In most cases, you're dealing with people who don't have that much talent and you really can't help them; but then there are always one or two people who will survive and who are very serious workers. Those you can help; you can show them what to do with a text. My real job is to take the writing and push it as far as it can go, without being cruel or judgmental.

FT: Would you say that the work of younger people has caused you to reconsider your own writing or affect it in any way?

JC: Very rarely. I really don't think I've found that, though I've seen some extraordinary student writing.

FT: To get back momentarily to the problems of publishing: I have the sense that editors have very little freedom of choice in what they do, and that they are frightened. I don't even know if there is an editor who is equal to certain texts. It's a real problem, apart from other considerations.

JC: Yes, it is a real problem, and I don't think that it was ever that different, but there was always a little bit more of a chance to do work that falls outside the boundaries. Maybe there will be again, and I'm not mourning. I just feel that the landscape has shifted and that I don't know where I belong anymore. I know I don't belong here.

FT: Do you feel that Paris is better for you in that regard?

JC: For the comic books, the graphic novels, it certainly is. I feel very much at home in Paris, and I love working with the publishers and the artists on these projects. It seems like there is no ego, no self-importance. They're not there to deal with "literature," they are there because they are people who have a certain expertise and who want to do the very best work they can. It's a pleasure to work with them. There's a wonderful energy in saying that you can do a novel in picture form with the same splendor, the same lyricism and emotional power.

FT: Maybe we should conclude with *The Magician's Wife*. It seems to me to be one of the most haunting books of the genre, and all the themes of your work, the brutality and nostalgia, seem to cohere in it.

JC: Of course you have to remember to give a great deal of credit to the artist [Francois Boucq]. But it gives me such pleasure to see words translated into these marvelous flowers, growing out of nowhere in some kind of wild landscape.

FT: Maybe out of the desert that you were talking about earlier?

JC: Out of the desert, yes. But I find it so strange that the French have taken a completely American form and found the means to do exciting, original work that we simply never could conceive of, that we don't have the imagination or technique to deal with. There's something strange about a form which is so utterly and completely American that has been stranded somewhere—lost, stalled, deracinated—and then picked up and altered into something we could never dream of doing. It's one of the things that drew me to France: the possibility of doing things there that I could never do here.

FT: Could you say a few last words about your involvement in theater?

JC: It came about as one of those fortuitous events. I never would have been able to work in the theater, but it so happened Mailer was the president of PEN, and I was a member of the executive board. He was kind enough to recommend me as a member of the Playwright/Directors Unit at the Actors Studio, and I began writing plays, sitting there working with Arthur Penn and Mailer and Elia Kazan, and it was a real education. Now, the Actors Studio is totally involved in naturalistic works, so my own theater pieces were bizarre and strange and didn't fit. But it didn't matter because somehow I was getting an education in the best sense of the word; I was going back to school.

FT: When did this occur?

JC: It began about four years ago. Arthur Penn was particularly wonderful in leading the classes, and I loved working with the actors. I've always loved actors, even as a kid. They've always been magical people to me, like idiot savants. When we were kids, we always thought the Actors Studio was a magical place, and here I was entering the temple, this strange usurper—again, the outlaw in the temple. I felt like an outlaw, but I did meet a few people who understood the crazy work that I was doing. The experience was enormously pleasurable, and I think it influenced books like *Paradise Man.* There is more dialogue in the later books, and that is partly because of dealing with dialogue on the stage. My own sense of theater was that it had nothing to do with words, but everything to do with choreography, with movement on the stage. So I wrote a play called *George*, about King George III, who is blind and deaf in his eightieth year. And his son, the Prince Regent, is a Jack the Ripper figure who goes through the palace holding up people because the king has left him penniless, with no allowance. The play was put on in Paris at the Maison des Ecrivains, and the French loved it.

FT: You mean, it was translated into French for the stage?

JC: Yes, and it was amazing to me. Suddenly, here is this play translated into French from another language, and the gestures of the actors, the interpretation of the director—they had understood the text! Here was my play in another language, and it was as if there had been no translation whatsoever.

Raiding the City:
An Interview with Jerome Charyn

Samuel Blumenfeld / 1992

From *Les Inrockuptibles* 35 (May 1992): 64–68. Reprinted by permission of Samuel Blumenfeld. Translated by Sophie Vallas.

SB: In *Metropolis*, you wrote: "Bronx boy, I grew up in a poor man's pile of streets, a ghetto called Morrisania."

JC: It's a very peculiar, very poor place. This ghetto had no equivalent. It gathered a lost and doomed people, and the children of those rascals were very special creatures: they were golems without past, present, or future. It would be very difficult for me to describe today the isolation I experienced in this ghetto. I did not read. You have to be very cautious when you used the word culture. If you live in Paris, you just have to walk for a few minutes to go from one neighborhood to another, but there are no neighborhoods in the Bronx, there are the immigrants and the others. The topography of such a place becomes visible thanks to the different ethnicities that compose it: the Jewish ghetto, the black ghetto, the Irish ghetto. Those people never really develop any relationships. The only rule that prevails in a ghetto is to get the hell out of it as soon as you have enough money to do so. Morrisania was a bedroom area. Without any future. It was nothing.

SB: What is left today of the place you grew up in?

JC: Nothing, the place no longer exists. All those areas where I grew up were destroyed. They built public housing projects and small individual houses for Latino immigrants to live in. The authorities thought that by doing so, those people would take better care of their neighborhoods! It feels very strange; I have no past I can go back to, I must either invent it or distort it. What is sure is that it's gone.

SB: Who were your parents?

JC: Immigrants who came from Eastern Europe. My father spent his childhood in a small town near Warsaw, and my mother lived close to Minsk, in Ukrainia. They practically never went to school. In the U.S., my father worked with a furrier. Just after the war the situation became very difficult for such a trade. So he started to spend most of his time at home while I was in school. It was very strange to grow up in such an atmosphere. My parents were unable to give me the keys necessary to understand the world I was about to enter. I studied Yiddish for a few years, but most of my education came from the street. For instance I had great difficulties learning how to read, and my father met similar difficulties just to understand English. In addition to that he had defective eyesight. As a child, because of an eye disease, he had to wait for two years before he could leave and join his family who had emigrated to the U.S. He was completely lost. He never had the opportunity to integrate into the American society. I feel like a diabolical son who decided to do something that his parents were never able to understand. I am a kind of saboteur who's neither American nor European and who belongs to several countries at the same time.

SB: Your novels make it obvious: almost all of them are situated in New York whereas you spend half of your time in Paris.

JC: I have no homeland; I only have two cities, New York and Paris. I really don't know if I am an American; I often don't feel very close to American culture. New York is much closer to a European country—or it used to be, I no longer know. I could find a calmness in Paris that doesn't exist in New York. Walking in this city sometimes looks like a dream. It's not so much the people or the culture of Paris that attract me as its topography, its places. And yet I don't think I could write about Paris with the same passion, the same fever, and especially not the same intimacy I feel for New York.

SB: What is your mother tongue?

JC: We used to speak Yiddish. My parents insisted that we exchanged a few words in English, but it was a most atypical English. I would say that, in fact, I had no language, neither English nor Yiddish. I only spoke a sort of grunting broken by many gestures and gesticulations. It was the language of a pantomime, I would say.

SB: Your novels are written in a language which is halfway between English and Yiddish, and they are not always within the reach of the average American reader. Is your language your homeland?

JC: Absolutely. There are elements in my novels that are accessible to some readers while they remain incomprehensible to others. I made the most of this situation which allowed me to compose my own dialect. When you have your own dialect, nobody speaks it, of course, but it constantly echoes in your ear. And in the end, your main interlocutor is yourself, and most of the conversations you have have nothing to do with the external world. A writer always has an internal voice. I would say that most of my readers are rather young, rather unconventional, and that they feel they belong to the margins of their own culture rather than to its center. It's a very particular audience of rebels who systematically refuse the frame that society offers them.

SB: Where did you learn to read?

JC: In comic books. Especially comics by Walt Disney, featuring Donald and his three nephews, Huey, Dewey and Louie. Then I started to read what was known as classic comics. Novels such as Dickens's *Great Expectations* were adapted and turned into comics, and it was for me the highest degree of culture. I love comics. Now that I write comic books, I have the sensation of going back to my roots. In the U.S., comic books have no cultural status. A comic book has no limits as far as inspiration is concerned; it never tries to stick to reality as most books do—with the exception of *Alice in Wonderland.* In most of the books written for children madness is very much under control. But in a comic book everything is allowed: you can suddenly go backward or forward in time, a character can be reborn or can turn into someone else. I feel very much comfortable in such a universe in which all frontiers are abolished.

SB: Reading *Movieland,* one can feel the importance of cinema in your childhood.

JC: My aesthetics comes from the comics, but my education comes from cinema. It's not only true for me—a whole generation had the same experience. The cinema was the only way I had to know what the adult world was like. The movies at the time never showed children, only adults who loved each other, hated each other, or killed each other. I was especially sensitive to the way those adults dressed and kissed. The movies showed an America I did not know, and it taught me to be a spy in the world of adults. Those movies were full of imagination, of romance, and above all of beautiful faces. No other cinema has ever disclosed faces such as the faces of Gary Cooper or Marlon Brando. You could only fall in love with such people. Their features were almost perfect. You were taught that love was something that could be very dangerous, but that it was essential at the same time. The movies also shaped my taste and my way of looking at the world. When you went to see a movie in those days, you could walk in the middle of a projection, and therefore I had to concentrate in order to try and understand what had happened in the beginning.

SB: In *Metropolis* you say that you are trapped in gangster movies.
JC: The gangster rebels against society and culture. I started rebelling against my surroundings from the moment I was born. I've always hated institutions, high school or college alike. Institutions always end up destroying what is particular and specific in an individual, and must therefore be fought. The gangster is at war with society, he doesn't work, he wears designer suits, he goes out with superb women, he has his own poetic language, and above all he has an amazing body language. Look at James Cagney in his first movies: whenever he walks he seems to be dancing. Take the ending of *Public Enemy*, for instance. When he dies in the rain, he looks like Fred Astaire or Gene Kelly in *Singin' in the Rain*. It's not simply a matter of showing off, it's a real symphony of the body.

SB: Is there a connection between the gangster, the immigrant, and the city?
JC: The gangster is the symbol of the immigrant who, as far as thinking and speaking are concerned, has never received a traditional education. The immigrant is the one who cannot find his place in the culture and in the society in which he arrives. He has no choice but to stand in the margin. And yet he has to find another way to integrate, by reinterpreting the signs that he receives. Most of the time he manages to do so by stealing and killing. He ends up acquiring a sense of responsibility, a certain culture. This is not only true for gangsters, by the way. When the first Irish immigrants arrived in New York at the end of the nineteenth century, they fought their way out by taking the key positions in the city, in the police and in the school system. In a way, they controlled the city. This is one of the reasons why New York is such a fascinating city: I don't know of any other city in which immigrants have constituted such a determining factor.

SB: Have you ever considered working for the cinema?
JC: I once was a scriptwriter, I even was an actor. I worked for Otto Preminger, but at a time when he was no longer powerful in Hollywood. It was a very frustrating experience because you have no control over the script you hand in. The producer and the director pretend that they need your talent and ideas, but in fact they simply want you to be their reflection.

SB: In *Metropolis* you compare yourself to Spinoza several times. And in *The Education of Patrick Silver* there is this rabbi who is a glass polisher, just like Spinoza. Are you both a Jew and an atheist?

JC: I have always been fascinated by Spinoza. I can still see myself at no more than ten—I couldn't find one of his books. I had to go all the way down to a black ghetto to find it. The librarian was the only white guy living in this ghetto. Spinoza is interesting because he had a vision of the world that clashed so radically with that of his contemporaries. He was excommunicated, excluded from his synagogue because he was an atheist. I was upset by this story, and for years I remained haunted by it. I don't feel I belong to a Jewish tradition, but in the end you make do with what you have, that is with your own story, and on the basis of this story you create your own mythology. I don't feel attracted to orthodoxy, rather to those people who came from Eastern Europe and ended up in America. They came with a sense of ethics, a sense of justice which previous to that moment had never existed in this country.

SB: You once published a book entitled *Arnold le geek de New York*. What's a geek?

JC: The geek is at the very bottom of the ladder. His role is to swallow chicken heads. He has no identity, no self-esteem. Being a geek is a nightmare but it's also a wonderful way to observe humanity.

SB: There are a considerable number of characters in your novels. Do you aim at competing with the Public Records Office, like Balzac?

JC: My work indeed is a kind of human comedy, but I think that the novel in general—and it goes beyond the case of Balzac—is interested essentially in characters. When I write, I never think of the number of characters that can coexist on a page. There is no logic prevailing; there are only situations that require these characters.

SB: The main character of your *romans noirs*, Isaac Sidel, is a cop who is far from being beyond reproach. On the other hand there are "baddies" who are not that bad. Do you write anti-*roman noirs*?

JC: I had never read any crime novels when I started writing one. I was much more influenced by writers such as Joyce or Faulkner than by the masters of the *roman noir*. I only started to read Chandler while working on *Blue Eyes*. Crime has become a central phenomenon in our society, so much so that today, a novel is, in a certain way, bound to be a detective novel. There is always a certain ambiguity in my books. One of the characters can be a good guy, but in the following volume he'll be a bad guy. A character in a novel moves in quicksand; it's never stable, it can change at any moment. The plot in my novels is always the same—it develops between people who have the power and others who don't have it. Except that those who think they have the power finally realize that they have, in fact, nothing at all. This is when a very particular dance begins, because nothing is ever certain.

SB: Corruption is very much present in your novels—Sammy Dune, the mayor of your New York City, is a good case in point. You used to be a close friend of Ed Koch's, who was the mayor of New York until 1988. Does the corruption you describe in your novels resemble the corruption in New York?

JC: Life in New York City depends on the Mafia, at least from an economic point of view. Without the Mafia, you can't read the *New York Times*. Transportation and housing are controlled by the Mafia. The authorities who run the city are essentially powerless and composed of incompetent people. I remain fascinated by the Mafia once again because of the dancer-type of gangster, his sense of eloquence, his eagerness to find another order in life. Everything's possible in New York if you can reach the right person. A mere phone call and your problem finds a solution. I remember going to the Yankee Stadium on the day of the opening of the baseball season. Everybody was there, deputy mayors, senators, secretaries of state, but when Mayor Ed Koch arrived everyone started hanging around him because at the time he was the one with decision-making powers. Have you read *The Government Inspector* by Gogol? It's the same thing in New York as in Russia. What must you do to obtain the right to serve alcohol in a pub? You just need to know the person who can pick up their telephone and get the authorization you want. I had tried to meet Ed Koch for a long time, with no success. Then I found the right person, someone who had a direct access to him, and, there you go, I had an appointment.

SB: Ed Koch was especially criticized as a mayor. And yet you seem to be very much attached to him.

JC: People accused him of being a racist, of ignoring the poor and the blacks. All this is true. Ed Koch was indeed a racist, and, up to a certain point, he was anti-black, but he was also a great mayor. He was available around the clock, he had almost no private life, and he got involved in the running of his city heart and soul. New York had never had such a mayor. Ed Koch was frightened by nothing—he was always ready to make new enemies, which is something I admire. I'd rather be represented by someone who fights than by someone who's constantly trying to smooth things over. Of course there was corruption around him—he even went as far as forging his own nickname, "the grocer of New York." He was a gangster in his own way, but a gangster who fought for his city. And I like that.

SB: What do you think about New York today?

JC: New York has always been the victim of the U.S. It's the city that pays the highest taxes in the country, in exchange for very poor compensations. In a period of economic crisis the problems cannot but worsen. The real test is taking place now: will New York City manage to educate its black and Hispanic populations? It's quite uncertain. It's still very difficult to know if those minorities will indeed integrate as well as the previous ones. The only solution to erase inequalities would be an educational program that gives opportunities to the youngest. They must be given a chance to understand the culture and the signs of the society they belong to. If I had remained in my ghetto, I would certainly have become a gangster, or a furrier at best. I was lucky enough to be sent to a special high school, where for the first time I met kids from the middle class. Unfortunately I'm no longer sure such a mixture is still possible today. I'm less a geek than a golem, someone who was made out of a clay that looks like no other, and who therefore had to somehow invent himself. Which is exactly the case of Ed Koch, and that's why I admire him so much. The guy turned his life into a legend. He used to be very shy, an introvert, but when he became a mayor, he went through a metamorphosis.

SB: You often compare the characters in your novels to golems. What is the difference between a golem individual and someone who isn't a golem?

JC: If you go back to the legend you'll see that the golem is a sort of monster created by a rabbi from the ghetto in order to protect the Jews from pogroms in the Middle Ages. The modern golem takes the shape of a city inside which we are all miniature golems. I think that more than in Europe or in America, my true origins are on Ellis Island, where the boats carrying the immigrants used to arrive. The golem's mission is to fight against evil— he has no heart, he has no soul, he is made out of clay, just like me.

SB: You depict Isaac Sidel like an omnipresent god watching over the whole of New York. Some say he is the real mayor of New York, others that he is the king of porn. Who is he exactly?

JC: I would say that he is the urban golem, sentimental and with no origins, both innocent and naive—a man who is ready to do anything in order to solve a problem. If you lived in New York you would need someone like Isaac to help you overcome your difficulties. Isaac is the one who must decipher signs, and in order to do that you must be ready and relentless. I did not invent Isaac—someone else must have in order to describe the mythology of New York City. To go back to your comparison with Balzac, I am writing the story of a particular species and Isaac just popped up on the page. I don't know whether you're familiar with chaos theories. Mathematicians and physicians have demonstrated that even disorder could be ordered. It seems to me that Isaac is the child of this chaos theory. The characters in my books have nothing to do with rationality. This may be one of the reasons why people find my novels difficult to read. And yet younger readers seem to have no problem, they're more supple. Take three sentences out of a novel: where is the link between the first one and the second, between the second and the third? There is no link. The blank space between two sentences is what matters; this is where reality is. I'm interested in this type of writing. It obliges you to read a book in another way. I wrote a text on George III, the king of England, and on his family. It's about a mythic England where the king's son is much closer to Jack the Ripper than to a prince. Is there a logic in all this? Yes, and this logic keeps being redefined, because everything is negotiable.

SB: Isaac Sidel lives with a tapeworm. Why?

JC: The worm stands for a sort of crazy manifestation of the urban world. Isaac keeps changing from one book to the next. In the first two novels he's really mean, and he only becomes a hero in the fourth one. He becomes a victim to the tapeworm only when his protégé is killed. He feels guilty about his death, and the worm is the internal presence of this external reality. He could get rid of it but he refuses to do so. The worm is the interior voice that everybody needs. In a way, Isaac comes from the Talmud; he is the man of the law.

Charyn, the Invention of Chaos

Serge Sanchez / 1993

From *Le Magazine Littéraire* 310 (May 1993): 116–18. Reprinted by permission of *Le Magazine Littéraire*. Translated by Sophie Vallas.

SS: You were born in the United States, the son of immigrants—a Polish father, a Russian mother. You are therefore at the crossroads of several cultures. What could you say about your family background, this melting pot in which your language developed?

JC: My parents did not speak English. We spoke Yiddish at home, and I spoke that language for a long time. Then came the language of the street. So I started to speak a sort of jargon, a hybrid language that was a mixture of those various influences. That's why I was attracted to James Joyce. But there were no books at home, and it took years before I finally learnt how to read.

SS: Precisely, do you think that the books one chooses, the books one loves, end up constituting a sort of family structure, a homeland?

JC: Yes, when you have no roots certain external echoes end up being part of your family. Such a belonging of course is a product of your imagination. And yet, in spite of this artificial dimension, the feelings that one may develop for certain characters—for Lolita for instance—are true. And they never leave you.

SS: Reading some of your interviews, one may have the impression that success brought you a feeling of guilt. You present yourself as a kind of monster.

JC: Which is true, especially as far as there was, in the beginning, a huge cultural void. This created this strange relationship that typically exists between immigrant parents and their children: the parents are the ones who need to be taken care of. And the children are the ones who teach their parents everything. In spite of this situation, the parents are still supposed to introduce their children to the world. But since they are not adapted to this very world, the children tend to withdraw into themselves and to reject whatever lies outside. I think this feeling of solitude, this introversion, may have been at the origin of my desire to become a writer.

SS: Do you remember the first books you read?

JC: *Pinocchio* came first. A thriller, already—Pinocchio is a bad boy. And then I read a lot of comics. What attracted me in comic books was the principle of the combination of images and words. As time went on, this led me to feel like having images burst out of words, like stupefying flowers. It's a little like Proust's madeleine, which contains a whole world. Before being a writer I was a painter. When I was six, I used to invent stories for myself and to draw the characters. I can still remember their very bright colors. Later on, I felt that painting did not allow me to express what I wanted, but that words did. So I put all my energy and efforts into becoming a writer. I devoted three or four years to this apprenticeship. But painting still haunts my books, just like cinema. As a kid, I used to go to the movies very often. I wasn't interested in the plot or in technics. What fascinated me was the magic of the close-up of a face talking on the screen. Even today, whenever I meet an actor or an actress, I can't help staring at them. I imagine close-ups of their faces on a screen.

SS: *Elsinore* is the title of your latest book and also the name of a nursing home. It sounds like a clear reference to *Hamlet*. In *The Catfish-Man*, Jerome is sent to an asylum and locked in the Bartleby pavilion. Is it another allusion to Melville?

JC: Yes, of course. There is an allusion to Melville in each one of my books. He's one of my masters. Reading Melville allowed me to realize that this feeling of "dislocation" that I had was not simply inside me, that the surrounding world was also subject to dislocation. In Melville's work human beings are just like stars, distant, removed from each other, scattered in the void. Now, how can you face the dark void around you? At one point in *Elsinore*, Sidney Holden, the hero, finds himself in a train station. He looks up at the ceiling and he sees the monstrous creatures of the zodiac that are drawn under the arches. "Taurus. Cancer. Capricorn. Aries with his horns and beard and big, big, eyes." Holden then wonders if he isn't just like them, "some night sign." And he feels like dying. It's a crucial scene. But no matter how serious books can be, humor must be kept in mind. Humor is also very important. I can find dislocation in the work of Henry James, a writer whose style I like a lot. And yet there are two things I blame James for. First his anti-

Semitism, although that's his own business. But above all, he's a snob. He is absolutely devoid of compassion, unlike Faulkner, Dostoevsky, or Melville.

SS: Your reflection on a dislocated world goes hand in hand with another theme in your work—chaos, which seems to be epitomized by the Bronx.

JC: Yes, chaos is a recurring theme. It is unconscious; it's like an eternal music which keeps being played. What I find so interesting in chaos is its organization. Chaos keeps turning into something else, reforming itself, undergoing metamorphoses. This notion of chaos is obvious in my style, but also in the plots of my stories. My characters change from one book to the next. They're not frozen, they are "changing landscapes." At the moment, I'm reading Isaac Bashevis Singer's *Scum*, which reminds me of Calvino and Borges. What I find extraordinary in this book are its elaborate systems of disorder, its dark patches of magic.

SS: In France, critics tend to put you on a shelf next to Chester Himes or Raymond Chandler.

JC: No, no, neither Himes nor Chandler. If you had to establish a connection with another *roman noir* writer, it would be Dashiell Hammett because of the aesthetic aspect of his writing. In fact, those I feel closest to are Rimbaud and Baudelaire, the precursors of the *noir* style. Their writing is violent. I used their influence in "1944," the first short story of *The Man Who Grew Younger*. Today, and this seems more and more obvious to me, I seem to be moving towards silence. The detective novel tends towards sobriety. It aims at the death of the text. I wrote for children too. It's a very interesting exercise which obliges you to be concise, to lay bare the language. I often wonder how literature can go through periods of amnesia. Beckett and Brecht, for instance, pushed their art extremely far. Today, people experiment too but without taking previous discoveries into account. I, for my part, struggle to prevent such influences from disappearing. If I was given only a hundred words I wouldn't feel limited at all, I would be able to write and to give life to a whole range of feelings. I am very interested in a language devoid of adjectives. I was also very influenced by Pinter, by these empty spaces that you can feel between his sentences. Such a vacuousness is a sort of revolution of language.

SS: In your books you often evoke chess, baseball. Are you a player?

JC: Yes, playing is an important dimension in my life. Ping-Pong, for instance. I spent two months playing against singer Georges Moustaki, whom

I met last summer. And at that time I stopped writing altogether. I was play-ing to win, not simply against someone but with the intention of beating them. I wanted to know what winning was all about. When I was younger, I played baseball and chess a lot. I even played in chess tournaments. If I had been good enough to go on, I would probably never have become a writer. I would have done like Duchamp, who stopped everything to devote his life to chess. In my books, games represent an element of organization. They symbolize order, but in fact, as far as chess is concerned for instance, the players constantly move in a very chaotic world. A world created by the strategy they invent. Nobody could beat Bobby Fischer because nobody could understand the universe his mind created.

SS: Why have you chosen Paris?

JC: I left the United States rather late, at thirty-six or so. When I arrived in Europe, the first city I visited was Madrid. Then I came to Paris and I thought "I'm finally home." It was like being in a dream. For instance I was unable to open the doors of the buildings. I didn't know you had to press a button to open them. I can't say exactly what in Paris attracts me so much. Its meandering streets, perhaps? And the Seine, of course. Crossing the Seine, walking on a bridge—there's something magic to it. When you go to the Île Saint-Louis, starting from Saint-Michel, you have to go over two bridges, and it's like a double passage that gives you access to an imaginary world. When I was younger, I used to live near the rue Mouffetard. Some-times I would remain locked in my room for several days, writing without going out. Watching down at the life below from my window was enough.

An Interior Journey into the Belly of the Beast: *Metropolis* by Jerome Charyn

Yann Lardeau / 1993

Originally published in *La ville et le cinéma*, Conseil Général de l'Ardèche (1993): 6–64. Copyright © 1993 by Le Conseil Général de l'Ardèche. Reprinted by permission of Le Conseil Général de l'Ardèche.

YL: Discussing the representation of the city in film always implies holding an architectural discourse on the cinema, which tends to limit it to its mere visual, pictorial, and somewhat decorative dimension. But in those films which are precisely built upon the sense of space—Fritz Lang's or Orson Welles's for instance—we notice that space is always blurred and incomprehensible. Therefore, I thought important, in introduction to this colloquy "The Documentary Film and the City" of the fourth symposium on the documentary (Etats Généraux du Documentaire), to contrast this architectural discourse on cities in film with a representation of the city that could also be an artistic creation—i.e., the creation of a subjective world where a city would mainly be viewed as a demographic event, a story of migrations, of cultural and ethnic shock encounters—in another medium than film—literature—where the notion of time is essential. To me, the cinema is first and foremost made of time and I thought it important to bring this basic component of the film to attention before any examination of the representation of the city in movies. It is also the reason why Jerome Charyn's participation in this colloquy seemed evident and essential to me. His work, *Metropolis*, is an essay on New York City. His description starts with Ellis Island, this island at the gate of New York—filmed by Georges Perec and Robert Bober in their 1979 *Récits d'Ellis Island*—which all the poor immigrants had to pass through before being admitted to the U.S.

Jerome Charyn, how did it occur to you to write *Metropolis* and why is Ellis Island so important to you since, to a certain extent, you consider it as the very center of New York City?

JC: Before I answer that question I would like to say that I was a bit surprised when I was invited to this festival because there is no logical connection between documentary and my book on New York. Then I realized that this search that I made about New York was really a film documentary, and it was confirmed last week when I was able to see *Route One/USA* by Robert Kramer, which upset me a lot. It was a great shock to see a very similar sensibility at work, and it confirmed my sense that the image was always locked inside the word. People began to call me crazy when I began to work on *bandes dessinées* in France, but I was the one who really understood that the image burst out of the word so that it was a natural progression for a writer to move from words into images. And those writers *très très snobs* who wouldn't consider the *bandes dessinées* as very important were not able to understand that this was the language of the future that very few people were able to understand, the sense of imagery in the world and the flowering of images through the word. And even though I can't consider myself as a kind of character within the book, in *Metropolis* it was really a kind of journey into the self and into the underbelly, the underworld of New York City. And even though Ellis Island in a way has disappeared from the sensibility of New York, and the immigrations of the eighties and the nineties are very different, Ellis Island was emblematic of the ideal of New York as the city of immigrants. And this was one reason, the main reason why New York was able to become such an incredibly energetic city: because it was able to redefine itself. It was interesting for me because I had no language as a child. I spoke no language, my parents spoke no language, so that, in a way, my intelligence or sensibility came from the street itself.

YL: How is it possible to represent a city from a point which is external to it? It seems to me, upon reading your novels as well as *Metropolis*, that every time you describe a population or a group or a city, we always stand in between two worlds: on the one hand the America of today and of yesterday—as being told through your characters—and on the other hand the ghosts of another world evoked in the story of the origins of each protagonist in your books.

JC: New York is a city of ghosts, it's a city of different pasts and it's a city of tribes. And we see the same tribalism now break out in Eastern Europe. It's something that can't really be explained, but it's so natural to our persona.

One thing I should also say in connection with the film you saw, *Récits d'Ellis Island*: it was only the very poor who arrived on Ellis Island. Those who had some kind of money and could pay first- or second-class passage never went through Ellis Island. They arrived directly in New York and were not investigated whether they had lice or eye-problems, etc. So you could see there was a very particular kind of prejudice that was not used against people who had an income, which is why in every sense it's a phantom island, and those people who arrived were also phantoms, as I am. Because if you asked me what my country was, I would have to say: it's Ellis Island. I am neither European nor American and I fit nowhere. And that's one of the reasons why my language is so difficult to describe, because it's not what you would call classic American—it's something else. It comes from another world. And that is the world I try to describe in my fictions and in *Metropolis*.

YL: Reading *Metropolis*, I found there is a particular mapping of the city which begins with Ellis Island and continues with Crotona Park, the mayor of New York (Ed Koch) and Harlem, and Chinatown. And each time, you have linked a district to a person or to a couple of persons who connect and create a typology of the people of New York City. How did you select those persons? Did you discard others? Did you start from the places or from the people?

JC: You have to remember that any book is part accident, and *Metropolis* was as defined by those people I could not see as by those I could see. I had my own Chinese connection, so I was able to deal with the Chinese Mafia, in the best sense and in the worst sense, and since my stockbroker was a former CIA agent from Korea, I was able to have access to the Koreans. But in reality, New York is a city of tribes, and unless you understand that tribalism and that sense of place, you have no access to the sensibility of New York. I happened to grow up in a particular area called Crotona Park, which, as Francis Ford Coppola would say, was "the asshole of the world." It was the place where everyone left and it was the place where I remained. In a way I have never been able to escape it in terms of my sensibility, so that is my greatest weakness but also my greatest strength.

Jean-Michel Paris: When I read your books, I have the feeling that Ellis Island stands like a center of gravity—the geographical center of New York City—but above all a human and intimate center of gravity to your own personal geography.

JC: Yes, Ellis Island is a kind of personal geography for me, but you have to understand it's not simply Ellis Island. It's what Ellis Island represents. Those immigrants who now come through Kennedy airport carry their own interior Ellis Island with them. And it is the same sense of displacement. So every time I go to an airport I freak out, because I feel like that emigrant coming from nowhere and going to no place. And I think that in order to understand New York, you have to comprehend this incredible movement, or migrations. Also the interior migration of blacks into Harlem, which has never really been discussed in the same way because it has been so poorly understood, but it was a very similar kind of immigration.

YL: In *Eisenhower, My Eisenhower* you depict a community of gypsies. In *The Education of Patrick Silver* and *Marilyn the Wild* we have Marranos who traveled through Peru, and we also find Polish Jews. *Paradise Man* stages Cuban immigrants. Each of these groups has its own mythology which is the transposition of an inner, utterly magical world. It is also something we find in *Metropolis*. How is it possible for someone from Eastern Europe, who carries their own mythology, to communicate or understand the mythology of the others? In other words, do the blacks from Harlem, the Chinese from Chinatown, the Russian or the Polish Jews from Crotona Parks live in isolated groups, locked in their own culture?

JC: These groups are totally isolated. They don't understand each other's language at all. Recently you could see the trouble between the Koreans and the blacks, as the Koreans have been very industrious, coming with entire families, and began to open little grocery stores throughout the city. Because it was a cash business, they almost paid no taxes at all. They kept their stores open twenty-four hours a day and no one could compete with them. They drove out the grocers of every other nationality. There was a tremendous problem between the blacks and the Koreans: the blacks felt completely exploited by these mad grocers who never closed, and the Koreans—not understanding these black creatures, why they didn't have the same industry as they did—became very defensive and there was a complete explosion, where the blacks began to boycott the Korean grocers and the mayor—who happens to be black—tried to create some kind of peace between these two communities. But it's really not possible. There is almost no communication between the tribes. The Latinos, for example, like to play on the fact that there is an identity between the Latinos (the Hispanics) and the blacks. They dislike each other and use each other as every other tribe. So, one of the profound sadnesses about New York is the isolation of these tribes. For example, even if you talk about the Latinos, you must separate them from the

Cubans. Because the Cubans who arrived from Havana were middle-class with an education and they immediately did very well in the United States. The passage from Cuba to the United States was very simple. Whereas those poor people from Puerto Rico were never able to make that sense of passage. And I only discovered that when I was teaching in one of the City Universities and found that my Latino students were as illiterate in Spanish as they were in English. So the only way I could teach them was through some kind of grunting and sign language and my own personal voodoo.

Michèle Gales: To me, New York City is Europe. I have always considered the communities of New York City like enclaves of solidarity and I find it great. I came to Europe because of this mixture of cultures which had fascinated me so much as a teenager. In Paris, midtown is the place where everyone wants to live and it is precisely the very contrary that occurs: people are being driven out of it. New York City is given as an example to explain that the pulling down of districts is not important, and to show that even in an inhuman surrounding and under the worst circumstances people manage to build this extraordinary exchange. I have my doubts. Midtown is the crossway where the people mix—a certain magic. If in Europe New York City is taken as an example to destroy the center of towns and drive people out, it is a very serious issue.

JC: Well, that's an interesting point because New York is really not an American city. It's really the Old World, the world of Europe reconstituted in some kind of fantasy. So that if you go to the *centre ville*, or midtown, it's a kind of ghost land of buildings, of skyscrapers that relate to no one and nothing. It's a landscape that's completely inhuman, which is surrounded by certain barrios, where the poor people live. And it's no longer a place that really works because the poor are only getting poorer, and at some point there is going to be an incredible explosion. You can already see this happening in Paris because it's so expensive to live there, people can't really start their lives anymore. So what happens in New York is a kind of training ground which happens later in the rest of the Western world—I am not talking about the East. The problems of New York, and what makes it so explosive and so powerful a myth, is that it is a training ground where the rest of the West can read its future. For example, New York was the first place where single people—those people who are not married, who live alone—became the great majority. So there were more single people than families. And now, it has already happened in Paris.

YL: When you create a novel in the world of Cuban immigrants or in the world of gypsies, do you reconstruct their mythological universe through documentation or is it a universe in which you project your own mythology—or is it a mixture of both?

JC: It's always a mixture, because the mythology is always truer than the literal facts. I wrote *Eisenhower, My Eisenhower* after living in California for three years and I didn't realize how lonely I was in California until one day I saw some mad person walking in the street of Palo Alto and I said: Ha! That's a New York face! I should also say that the title of the novel would not be understood by anyone because it comes from a particular jacket, which was called "the Eisenhower jacket" and which was worn by soldiers in World War II. And it is the only thing I wore for fifteen years. The important thing is that I wrote that book and it is really the first book where I discovered my own style. I wrote it after coming back from California and living in New York, and it is about a tribe of gypsies who have tails and they make love with their tails. For me they represented the other, the outsider, the blacks, the Jews, all those people who didn't fit. And it was my revenge upon the rest of the world, because suddenly these gypsies who had no power—and by the way they live in a city called Bedlam—began a revolution against the Anglos, the WASPs. Their secret hiding place was inside the bowels of a garbage truck. That's why nobody could find them. Like all the other minorities, they gradually began to take over the city, and when they took it over, they discovered they had nothing at all! Which is the saddest mythology of our time. You could see this in New York with the Irish, with the Jews, and the blacks. The Irish were the first ones to replace the native culture, that is, those WASPs who controlled New York. The Irish threw them out, controlled the city, and became the greatest thieves in the universe. The contribution that the Jews made in the beginning of the century was that they added a kind of moral politics, a sense of social being that had not been there before. As soon as they entered politics—and we had a Jewish mayor for the first time only in the 1970s—they became ultra conservative and thieves like anybody else. Now we have a black mayor, with black commissioners, and we are undergoing the very same problem. So God help those who come to power!

Public: In France, we believe that the American government is much more concerned by international politics rather than social and domestic affairs.

JC: No, no. There is a relationship between the external politics that is going on now and the internal politics of the country. I mean the Republican convention, for example, in a way is the mirror to what is happening in New York. For example the gays in the United States first acquired a kind of power in New York City. And the Republicans don't know what to do, what should be their stand, with or for or against the gays. So you see this marvelous president saying that if he had a relative who was gay he would not be against that person, he would accept him or her as part of the family. You could see the same prejudice worked out in the rest of the country as it has already been worked out in New York City. Again, New York City becomes a mirror for the rest of the world—since the United States is part of the world, it also has to be included, unfortunately. I should also say that, I am afraid, as an American and a New Yorker, as soon as I leave New York I really get frightened because I don't understand the sensibility of the way people behave. I don't understand their language and it really frightens me. There is a lack of humor and that is very disturbing to me.

Cécile Bloc-Rodot: My question is about the connection between documentary films and the city. You are a novelist. What did you feel when you wrote a documentary book about the town where you were born and where you grew up? What did you feel as regards the voice, the eye, the style?

JC: That's a very good question and a very difficult question to answer because you discover the eye and the style only through the text that you are writing. So I did not have this eye and this style when I began writing *Metropolis*. I had to discover it in the book and in my own way I felt like a little Marco Polo going to China, discovering the wonders of spaghetti. So that, when I wrote this book, I had to invent an eye and a style. And it came through the ear: I had to find the music and the imagery that would go with the images and the thoughts. So, as I was a child who had no language—and in the book I say that the writer takes his revenge upon the world through his language, through his own particular silence—the most powerful thing for me is the feeling of silence. To be able to say what finally can't be said. And I had my father in mind when I wrote this book because he has no language at all, and I had to enter the city as if I were an outsider, because if I were inside the landscape, I couldn't have found the language for the book. It's not a novel, and it's not journalism, it's a kind of interior journey into the belly of the beast.

Public: The question is about your sense of panic and displacement in airports. You said you had the feeling of being like an emigrant coming from nowhere and going to no place. Twice you said that your parents had no language. Is it a problem of identity that you carry with you, in your mind, in your suitcase, in the airports?

JC: Yes, again it's a very good question. My parents came from Poland and Russia. They never had a chance to really learn English and my dilemma was that my father, who spoke no English, had to teach English to me. So we would sit for hours when I was five, six, or seven and go over long lists of words that I couldn't understand or pronounce. So that language itself was always a kind of magic for me. And words had a kind of feeling because the only way I could interpret them was through the image. An airport anywhere has no real language. It has signs, it has a sense of direction, but it does not have any kind of interior life.

YL: You are a true film buff and you called your book about New York *Metropolis*, like Fritz Lang's film. Something really strikes me: at least in Lang's first films (the series of *Mabuse* or *Spies* for instance) we don't really know where the characters live. They live hidden in hotels; they work in concealed offices. They are always disguised. We never know what their real faces are. I find something of the same order when I read your novels: the characters have no fixed address, they move, they are disguised, etc.

JC: I think everyone talks about Fritz Lang's German films but in a way his American films are even more interesting. They are not as great because they don't have a central language, but they are unique, they have a unique signature. They remain very disturbing to me because they have no real address. And this is something that has always interested me about New York and it is becoming more and more critical as there are more and more homeless people. There was a landmark case in New York City that was fought out by a man who claimed that his address was a certain bench at Central Park. And he won the case. Therefore he was able to get all the benefits that the city could give because that bench was where he lived.

Marco Venturi: Could you say a few words about the role of space in your books? Apparently you only deal with myths, mythologies, tribes, social behaviors. At the same time, you said that you still live in the same place where you grew up even if the lifestyle and the places have changed, if the people who now live there are no longer the same. There is one thing I don't understand: is the city a space or is it a set of behaviors? And if it is so, why are you still attached to places rather than to behaviors or myths?

JC: Well, if you mean place as New York City, then I would say that no matter where I live—and I happen to be living in Paris now—I could not really interpret the mythology of Paris. And the only mythology I can really comprehend from the interior is this phantom mythology of New York City where place and address don't really matter, because they constantly change. So even when I begin a book—which is also a sense of place as you write a book—I feel as if I am falling in a kind of quicksand. That's what makes the writing of the book so interesting. As you gather the power of language, you also disappear. New York is a place like any other place—90 percent of the time, its ingredients would be the ingredients of any city. But it is the other 10 percent that really gives it its particular flavor and its particular power. For example, you have Fifth Avenue and Park Avenue which don't change at all, but for me it's a kind of golden grave. The real places that are in constant flux, where immigrants come and are then replaced by other waves of immigrants, they are the ones who represent the real sense of a city, particularly when we talk about crime, because at the heart of any modern city is its criminality. For example New York City is completely unworkable without the Mafia. It is the Mafia which is the real government of New York City. Everybody knows it but no one wants to talk about it.

Public: What are the links between the Mafia and Wall Street?
JC: There is no difference. Most of the so-called money is laundered money; it is dirty money that is put into banks, then reinvested, and that finally goes back into Wall Street. So that the black market or the grey market is the real market that matters. And for example you can go into many shops on Madison Avenue where there are never any customers whatsoever, and these are laundering operations for the Mafia. It means taking money, putting it into legal businesses, and then getting the money out. Again, no one wants to talk about it. No building could get built without the Mafia. They control all the unions and I will give you a particular example: there is one union that is involved with putting in windows, and only putting in windows. So you could put your building up but you wouldn't have any windows, and that's the story of the Mafia. And by the way, there are never any strikes.

YL: Your brother Harvey, who is a policeman, is a very important character in your books. In what ways does his vision of New York differ from yours? How does he consider New York and what does he think of your novels?
JC: My older brother was very important to me. He is three years older than I am. And I could only describe him as a gentle killer, because like most policemen he's also a killer. When I began to write so-called "crime

novels," when I was very naive, I went to these police stations and worked with detectives, several of whom were mental cases from Vietnam. I only really understood what they were about when I began to move around with this policemen who really could relate to no one except other policemen and their own stool pigeons and also other criminals. Because they all spoke the same language. And there was a peculiar combination of aggression and shyness at the same time. It's no accident that the highest suicide rate is among policemen because they are used up. They can really not relate to the outside world. They have their own language, their own sensitivity. For example, I don't know if any of you are familiar with the Mafia figure called John Gotti, who was the most powerful Mafia figure and still is. I happened to attend his trial and my brother was testifying at his trial because he is a Mafia expert. I went with him from a ceremony where he was promoted to second-grade detective. He was wearing his uniform, and he had to stop off at his office. I asked him why. He said because he wouldn't appear before Gotti in his uniform; he had no wear his own fancy clothes. He went into his locker and suddenly there was this incredible transformation: a kind of George Raft figure emerged from the locker room with a suit, a hand-painted beautiful tie, and a white-white shirt, beautiful shoes, and these were his court clothes. And he wore them for John Gotti!

Public: I have a very different question which is connected to the work that is done in Lussas on documentary films. I would like to know if you have ever thought of making films and, if so, would they be fictions or documentaries?

JC: Yes, I am very much interested in films. I have written for the cinema, but I am even more interested in documentaries. I am preparing a documentary, but it would be premature to talk about it. It's a form that I really love, and it's in a way a very perverse form because all documentaries are really fictions and all fictions are really documentaries. The most powerful cinema fictions really rise out of documentaries. And it's sad for me that documentaries in the United States are so rarely seen on the screen.

Public: Has the character of John Gotti influenced *The Good Policeman*?

JC: Oh yes, yes. The godfather, Jerry Di Angelis—he is the godfather in *The Good Policeman*—was very much influenced by the character of John Gotti. I remember when I was at his trial, and I came in—I was the only face he didn't know in all the courtroom. And as I came in with my brother, he must have assumed I was some kind of secret super CIA/FBI agent, so secret that the whole courtroom was frightened and oblivious of this character, and I acted out this fantasy by looking at him straight in the eyes. And so as you say in English, we eyeballed each other for about five minutes, and I must say he is the most fearless person I have ever seen in my life. I, who had the advantage of mystery, had to look away first. So there's no way that that man could be scared, and that's his real power. For example, when he went to jail, he made up this little jingle and he said, "Ready for Freddy," which can't be translated into French. He was ready to go to jail—it didn't matter! He was ready for anything. Also in the 1970s I wrote four crime novels which were all very much influenced by my own relationship with my brother. So every time I wrote a book, I would call him on the phone. And then there was a fifteen-, sixteen-year interlude between writing about the same characters, but it was the writing of *Metropolis*, about New York City, that made the real difference between those first four books and the next four books that are going to come. And you realize that you use your entire life when you build up any kind of narrative or fiction. You're using things that may have happened to you when you were four years old. Because I met Ed Koch, the mayor of New York, and spent some time with him, I was able to use those experiences in the writing of these crime books which have a much more direct relationship with the city itself.

YL: Nine years ago I interviewed Lillian Gish and I asked her how Griffith had reacted to the arrival of sound films. As a matter of fact, Griffith had already shot a sound film in 1921, *Dream Street*, which had been played at the Town Hall in New York, on Forty-third Street, in one of those giant theatres which were open twenty-four hours a day and held more than five thousand people. The immigrants learnt English reading the inserts. Griffith (who happened to be in the theatre) saw all the people leave because they could not understand the film any longer, and he thought: "This is suicide, I'm losing my audience because they can't speak English." Five percent of the world's population spoke English at that time, which meant that he would lose 95 percent of his audience. But Jack Warner was also in the theater and he just thought the opposite: "This is the future of cinema." When I read *Movieland*, and when I consider the importance of the movies in your books, I feel that cinema stands for a kind of double of New York and for an imaginary language which allows one to find an identity.

JC: Unfortunately Griffith was wrong. Like all the people of my generation I grew up at the movies. But it was very particular because from the moment I was a child until I was fifteen I never once came into the cinema at the beginning of a film. I always entered in the middle of a film and that's a tremendous advantage because I grew very clever at the movies. I began to interpret very quickly what was going on, and I knew the first part of the film without having to see it. And of course at that time there were always two films, not one. So, when you went to the movies, you were completely exhausted because you were sitting there for five hours. And I always went during the day, not in the evening. So I would go in around one, come out around six o'clock, and it was already dark in the winter. The day had completely disappeared, but at the same time I had made such startling discoveries that it was worth it. Also I never knew the names of the directors because the credits didn't matter. Who cared? The only thing that mattered was the actors, and subliminally it was the photography of course, it was the close-ups. It wasn't the action. I didn't care who killed whom. So when you saw Gary Cooper's face, and particularly when he was in love, and he was always in love—that's what films were all about.

To Write Is to Die a Little:
An Interview with Jerome Charyn

Sylvaine Pasquier / 1994

From *L'Express* (29 September 1994): 98–117. Reprinted by permission of Le Groupe Express. Translated by Sophie Vallas.

SP: You have two cities in your life—New York, which haunts your whole work, and Paris, where you live now. How do you manage this double passion?

JC: Do you remember *Pépé le Moko*? There's a scene in this movie when the heroine, this blond girl who's just arrived in the Casbah, asks Pépé if he knows Paris. "Paris is my last hole," he says. These words hold true for me too. Paris is indeed my last hole, my spiritual home. Paris is a voice, a voice that speaks to me and that soothes me when I walk on its streets. In other words, New York was driving me crazy. It's a schizophrenic world where everyone is free to be anything. At one point I suddenly saw the person I was developing into and it wasn't the person I wanted to become. I love New York as much as I hate it. This city was bringing me death. Being away from it does not mean ceasing to write about it, whether better or worse—it doesn't matter. And yet, even if I was told that I wouldn't be able to finish a novel in Paris, I would stay here. The enchantment I experience here is too great. I'm so attached to it, it's as if my life now depended on it.

SP: What is the reason for such an enchantment?

JC: The space. I was becoming claustrophobic in New York—this impression of being at the bottom of an abyss, surrounded by vertiginous walls. Such heights have nothing to do with the human. Whereas Paris bathes in an amazing flood of space, as if the buildings were ships floating on the ground. It's very lyrical for me. And the balconies, the lines of the balconies on the facades. They look like the staves and barlines on a partition. I couldn't live

50

in a building or a room without balconies. They structure a view, they give it a magical frame. It would be useless to look for such a thing in New York. Anyway, my hometown was the worst place for me to live in.

SP: Why?

JC: That's something I understood the first time I came to Europe. In Europe there's a sense of the past, even a way of stressing the presence of the past, which I really need—even if I wasn't conscious of it before. The United States live in the constant tension of an eternal present. It's a schizophrenic universe that was turning me into a geek—you know, the guy who tears off chicken heads with his teeth on fairs. When I reached that point I was no longer sure I was human anymore. I was looking for something I knew nothing about.

SP: Why are you so faithful to some of your characters, and especially to Isaac Sidel, the "red commish?"

JC: It wasn't my intention to write more than one novel about him. He's probably a fantastic go-between. This supercop who's considered as the real mayor of New York haunts the nine circles of hell. He knows everyone and all the wastelands. When Blue Eyes got killed, his ghost took possession of Isaac's stomach in the shape of a tapeworm. And the "Commish" became an uninterrupted melody to me. I feel very close to him. One of his problems is that he's unable to understand who he is—that is, both American and European. Isaac cries easily. He is obsessed by a woman that a police chef should avoid like the plague: she works both for the FBI and for the KGB. He spent three months with her, in school, forty years earlier. She was born on the ruins of the Nazi lunacy. She is a wreck, and yet she manages to retrieve the sense of what a human being is. She's this voice emerging from the surrounding chaos which Isaac is desperately in love with. Because he too is a creature of history, and because he suffers from its absence.

SP: Some of your characters have their own appointed rabbis, who are not precisely mainstays of their synagogues.

JC: A rabbi is essential. He has the power to magically solve any of your problems. The term comes directly from the slang used by the police—a world in which political supports are determining. In other words without a rabbi you'll never get a promotion. I was my brother's rabbi for a while, when he worked for the homicide squad in New York, simply because I had become friends with several commissioners.

SP: Do *you* have a rabbi?

JC: Every one of us should have one. A rabbi's your guide, your champion, your voice—a coherent voice. My only rabbi is the text, the words in the text. One of the reasons that pushed me to write was that I was unable to speak. I could only grunt incomprehensible words. At the university I found myself sitting next to rather strange students. Four or five among them would become Nobel Prize winners. They expressed themselves with such dazzling clarity. Whenever I listened to them, I would freeze on the spot, and the only possible revenge was for me to grab hold of a sheet of paper. There I was at least more coherent. I could speak to myself, not with sounds but with written signs. I had to transpose the music of sounds into writing.

SP: Why do you say that the writer is a gangster?

JC: Language is terribly cruel. The words have their own point of view; this should never be forgotten. It's precisely what the political correctness that's fashionable in the U.S. at the moment is trying to negate: banishing expressions or imposing others only results in perverting language. Those voluntarist simplifications will never prevent it from being irrational, complex, impossible to master. Language can do anything. The gangster and the writer share a similar relationship with irrationality. The former exploits the irrationality of men, and the latter that of words. For both of them irrationality is a fearsome weapon, provided that they keep a firm hold on it. Faulkner was one of the first to take that road. He got as close as possible to the dangerous zone while neutralizing its destructive potential. In my opinion language can kill. Stalin knew that better than anybody else. He perfectly understood the power of words as well as the threat they represented for him. Because he could not subject them to his will, he imagined that by crushing the writers he would crush the words.

SP: Are you aware of the risks you submit your reader to?

JC: There is no such thing as an innocent reader. The reader is part and parcel of the whole thing! The act of writing is probably immoral in itself, but it's also the most moral act there is since you derive no benefit from it. You just kill yourself, that's all. I always burst out laughing whenever I hear a director or an actor saying, as they're retiring: "This job is exhausting. I'm going to write a book." Well, go on, treat yourself! Sometimes I feel as knocked out as a boxer pelted with too many blows.

SP: Is it always that painful?

JC: Always. There's no such thing as a book you easily finish off, or then it's a worthless book. I spend my whole time chasing words that slip away. But I'm stubborn. I write in the same way I play Ping-Pong. It's exactly the same.

SP: Are you a good player?

JC: I never learnt how to play, my style is bizarre, my service could be better, but I put an amazing concentration in it. When my opponents feel close to victory, they often drop their guard. That's when I overcome my handicap and I win. It's a matter of vigilance. Ideas are just like balls. They fall on you unexpectedly and slip through your fingers if you have a moment's inattention. All the New York Ping-Pong clubs have disappeared. Here in Paris I go to a club run by the subway workers of Paris, in the 13th Arrondissement. I go there every day. Most of the time, I play against Georges Moustaki or against a jockey who's a real virtuoso. I almost always lose—it's the only way to learn. When I started reading Joyce, I knew that I would never write a sentence endowed with such beauty, such might, such melody. But I could try and find my own road. You finally succeed after you've learnt to overcome a feeling of failure.

SP: How did you discover your own road?

JC: Strangely Freud was the writer who influenced me the most. When I read *Moses and Monotheism* I was struck by the fact that he calls Moses "the Egyptian," and it opened new perspectives. In one word he disclosed a whole deep, invisible structure. I am no philosopher. But on that day I understood that the strangest connections are sometimes not the least justified.

SP: Could you expand a little?

JC: I'm thinking of what I owe my brother. For years he was the embodiment of sadness. And whenever he was obliged to commit a deed that was much worse than what he was naturally capable of, this sadness increased. Because you know, I don't want to overdo it, but there is no real difference between the police and the criminals. They come from the same background, and all of them are gangsters. Every other decade a huge scandal in the ranks of the police confirms this. I mean, among the cops also, if there's money to be made. In the end the cops have simply legalized the outlaws—in New York, at least, and maybe only in New York, it doesn't matter. There has always been a common ground between cops and criminals. The Mafia had its blocks, its neighborhoods, which the police would never enter, and vice versa. In this way they managed to establish a form or order. As soon as the

Federals turned up to clean the whole place, chaos came back. Today the only calm and crimeless neighborhoods—such as Pleasant Avenue, the only Italian street in Harlem—are those that the Mafia still controls. But their territory is no longer what it used to be.

SP: Who is trying to take over?

JC: The Chinese, the Russians, or others who will probably be less organized and much more destabilizing than the Italians. The Italians, at least, had a certain sense of aestheticism as well as the elegance to assassinate each other. My brother was an expert on the Mafia. When I was doing research for *Blue Eyes* and *Marilyn the Wild*, he took me to Bath Beach, an Italian neighborhood under control. We went into a restaurant—everyone instantly fell silent. They knew he was a cop, they thought I was one too. Everyone was strangely affable towards us, and we could feel fear underneath. This was enough, at the time, to hold chaos in check. But today . . .

SP: The gangs that now dominate your natal Bronx have forgotten what fear is.

JC: I thought I knew this borough. I went back there recently, taking the opportunity of a script on those freelance reporters who work every night for television channels. It's no longer possible to say that it's a jungle—the word supposes a form of brutal beauty. No, it's a dead jungle. If nothing changes, war will soon invade the whole city. The most serious problem New York—and probably the U.S.—has to face is that the city is now unable to give an education to the youth. Half of the schools of the country are now equipped with detectors to prevent the kids from bringing their guns in class. Who could study in such conditions? Eleven-year-old kids commit murders. They are born in an apocalyptic world. They go to schools that are besieged. How could they know what the word *human* means?

SP: Why has New York become the wild city, "la ville sauvage par excellence," as one of your latest books asserts?

JC: Because it's the only metropolis in the world that loomed up from the dregs of society. At the end of the nineteenth century it was the scene of a real battle waged by the poorest—the Irish, who gave birth to the first modern gangs—to defend their positions in the city. And the rich lost their power. In other words they still controlled Wall Street and the banks, but they had lost the political scene. New York is the only city in which the most destitute found a way to educate themselves and to dislodge the well-off.

It's a historical fact. Because I wrote about it, I am now blamed for being the spokesman of the poor. But the rich have their own spokesmen, who are numerous enough. They don't need me. In other words I dance with the misfits and the drop-outs, and not with the mighty. When I used to teach in Stanford, I lived close to San Francisco for a while. I was missing something, and I was powerless to know what, until one day I saw a man walking on the street and talking to himself. In California nobody behaves like this. Everyone behaves in a very rational, controlled, and polite way. It drove me crazy. And yet I love to go to Hollywood. But not under any circumstances.

SP: What do you mean?

JC: When I'm working on a scenario, I settle in a hotel room, on the twentieth floor. This is where I receive the people I have appointments with, where I eat, and from where I order the videos I need. I never set foot outside, not even once. The surrounding city looks like a jungle to me. It's a fantastic city provided that you don't stay there more than a week.

SP: Why did you give feminine first names to the two male characters of your latest novels?

JC: What I'm trying to suggest without insisting too much on it is that everyone is more or less androgynous. Men are supposed to be tough and women to be tender creatures, whereas you can say the exact opposite in many cases. In this period of strange madness such gendered statements are meaningless. On the other end we have a desperate need for the feminine side of humanity, or at least for the values this side is supposed to embody. The twentieth century has kept glorifying macho barbarity, and if we launch into the next century with such a brutal way of looking at the world, I wouldn't put too much money on our survival.

SP: When you chose to live on this side of the Atlantic, were you aware that you were coming back to the continent your parents had left?

JC: What I know is that today, for the very first time, I can write on my mother. I have a few photographs of her. I change them into words, and I change the words into images. It's the only dialogue I've been able to establish since she died. Four months ago I was in Hamburg and I was aimlessly wandering in the town. I happened to reach the harbor. I was shown where the docks were. And there, I suddenly realized that my mother had walked those quays, those wooden piers. Coming from Russia and after a long journey, she had reached Hamburg and embarked on the boat to the U.S.

SP: Hadn't you tried to see the place before?

JC: I had never consciously thought about it. And suddenly, this emotion. Hamburg invented my mythology.

SP: Would you say that Europe is giving back to you the missing links of your past?

JC: Perhaps. I had to live in France to start feeling compassion for my parents, for instance. For years I had been angry at them for having no sense of language. They remained powerless to master the signs of the New World because they could not understand English. When I arrived in Paris, I found myself in the very same situation. Today I speak an elementary French, but I would be unable to express anything complex in this language. When I listen to kids speaking on a bus, I am eaten up by jealousy. They will ultimately discover what will always remain elusive to me: the music of the language.

SP: What are you working on right now?

JC: I'm working on a rather strange, three-hundred-page comic book, *New York 1999*, for an American publisher. And I'm setting a precedent since I'm the first writer to retain the rights over his own characters. What is paradoxical is that the U.S. would never have offered me this possibility if I hadn't already experienced it in France. The volumes I co-wrote with Loustal and François Boucq have enthralled American people. Once again, as for the cinema or the *roman noir*, the French taught them that comic books were a form of art.

SP: Perhaps living here will allow you to find your true place in the U.S.

JC: I think so. It's probably a matter of believing, just as Marco Polo did, that wherever you go, you have something to do there. And yet it's strange. France has offered me experiences. It has allowed me to live as a writer. And if Paris is so important to me, it is also because the city endlessly lends itself to this very adventure that used to be my passion when I lived in the Bronx. In the Bronx, I used to live between two hills, and the great challenge was to go on top of them to see what was beyond. In Paris you just have to turn a corner, and suddenly you're entering a different world. The city is telling you a story. And all the storytellers have had the same mission ever since the mists of time: to absorb the suffering of mankind and to find a way to soothe it.

"Desperately Seeking for the Undersong": A Definition of Voice by Jerome Charyn

LOLITA (Laboratoire Orléans-Tours de Littérature Américaine) / 1994

From *GRAAT* 12, *Effets de voix* (1994): 41–45. Reprinted by permission of Trevor Harris.

JC: I'm struck by something Roland Barthes said in *Writing Degree Zero*, that twentieth-century language exists outside of culture and history, and is a language full of dream and menace. I think the dream and menace are really where Pynchon and Barthelme and other writers of that order exist. It's a kind of dreamspeak; I knew Barthelme quite well and met Pynchon without ever knowing it because you were not introduced to Pynchon. One is struck by the eternal sadness underlying the comedy, and I think that's certainly true of Barthelme in particular; how to describe the language or the voice or I would say the undersong, and that is, you read with a kind of internal ear and your ear picks up the song in the language, and to me that is the voice.

I would say that one's life has a particular song; you find a rhythm and you're graced with that rhythm and you move into it and you move out of it, and I think it exists beyond irony, I think it exists beyond meaning, it exists in images, metaphors, and it's something that is *so* difficult to talk about, it seems to me, it doesn't matter whose work it is, but to talk about voice, it's so primitive, it's so elementary, it's so essential to the text that it's quite difficult to grasp.

Marc Chénetier: That wraps it up pretty well! Just to launch into the discussion, two questions that are very different: One: In *Pinocchio's Nose*, there is a whole passage on what you call "mythopsychosis." Mythopsychosis, the way I understand it, is merging into somebody else's character and trying to come out with his/her voice. So, could you expatiate on this? Two: Nobody in your books ever walks into a room, goes into a room, he either dances or waltzes or flies: now, what is the relationship of this to the tonality that you're trying to establish?

JC: Mythopsychosis, in my mind, is the disease that causes us to narrativize everything. If you put three words on a blackboard, we would necessarily, in terms of our own life, have to form a narrative around the three words. I think we narrativize everything, in terms of meeting someone, we narrativize a relationship; it's more than fantasizing, it's this illness, the desire and the need, the desperate urge to tell a story. So I would say that all writers, good or bad, suffer from a kind of mythopsychosis, which is the need to narrativize their own lives. I always shy away from meaning, I don't care what the meaning of the text is, I care what the music is because the meaning will come from that music. Faulkner is a profound writer because he allows you in his music to get so close to his characters that it's quite frightening, and it's that kind of proximity that provides the meaning.

In relation to your second question, yes, because someone just wrote a paper called "Waltzing with the Witches," which is about the idea of dancing in all these strange texts of mine. I didn't notice it myself until I went back and saw that characters always do waltz into a room, or they're constantly dancing. For example the novel that I've just completed is called *Death of a Tango King*, and again, there's this constant desire to exist within the frame of the dance, which is the frame of the music of the text, and it seems to me that it's always in relation to a song. I'm not saying that it's true of any other kind of writing, but I'm saying that *when I read a text, it's not the meaning that holds me, it's the need to find the song, and if I can't find the song in the first page, I don't read the second page*; I must hear that music in my own ear. I must hear that waltzing, I must hear that kind of dancing which you get constantly, let's say from Faulkner in the very first image of *The Sound and the Fury*; you're just stuck in the music and you can't get out of it. And it's certainly true of Nabokov. It starts with James Joyce and maybe *all* of modern writing comes from those first lines of *Portrait of the Artist*: "Once upon a time and a very good time it was . . . ," suddenly taking you *into* the narrative and into its song. I would call it the undersong, I look for the undersong when I start a text. What is the music that underlies the narrative, never mind the meaning, what is the music? And for Barthelme, it would be the incredible sadness that underlies every single text of his, that ultimate, terrifying kind of pessimism that is coupled with this incredible music and imagery.

Marc Chénetier: The last word you used is a way of relaunching the discussion. What is it that produces the song you're looking for? Where do you spot the first modulations of it, is it metaphor, is it something that raises the text above itself in some manner or another, is it rhythm?

JC: I think it's rhythm, and metaphor, and certain writers have it in an infinite way: Bill Gass has never written a bad sentence—you can't find it—so in a sense when you read Gass, whether it's his essay on the color blue, I mean they're all fictions, it doesn't matter what is a fiction. I was just talking to Marc before about trying to punish him because Gass's essay hasn't been translated into French and he's saying that you can't find any equivalent for the color blue or the permutations of the color blue, but that is such an elemental text about modern writing that it *has* to be translated—and perhaps it can't be; but I would say that I don't know what the magic tone is, whether it comes from the metaphors; but when I read Grace Paley, I *hear* something in my ear that I don't when I read writer X, Y, or Z. When I read Cynthia Ozick, I *hear* from text to text, from line to line, from image to image, from mood to mood, a kind of tonality that's like a stream of language which Barthelme writes about in one of his stories.

Now, Barthelme is something else. It's a kind of broken syntax, it's a kind of schizoid landscape that bombards you with images and pulls at you in every direction, with its incredible intelligence, with its ability to throw back the culture at you on all its permutations, taking all the junk food of language, playing with it, twisting it around, with infinite pleasure at the same time; he's incomparable, I think he changed the whole landscape of sixties fiction, and it's sad to me that a writer of that power has not found the audience that he deserves, because he defined the whole sensibility of the sixties in the United States more than any other writer.

Noëlle Batt: In fact you've just changed the metaphor: instead of having voice, now we have music! And when you try to define it you use words like metaphor, rhythm, mood.

JC: Because it's so difficult. I can't equate Barthelme's music with Gass's music, it's not the same, they're almost the opposite: one has a very profound, beautiful, regular modulation, the other has a very schizoid, tight pause in its structure, but they both have very distinct voices. You can recognize them, almost by reading two lines. Just pick them up and you can tell it's Barthelme even though it's true that there were Barthelme clones existing almost as soon as there was Barthelme. There were other people sending out stories in his name and I remember him telling me—because I thought it's wonderful, "Look, it's great to have all these imitators, don't you feel great?" and he said, "No, I'm not getting their checks!"

Also, the other question I find fascinating is that when you read a writer and you hear him or her speak, then when you go back to their text, you're reading it in a much different way because you can hear the inner voice and it's incredibly more pleasurable. When I read Barthelme now, I can always hear the sound of his voice, so I would say it has to go back to the spoken word, and in a way this was what the Voice Project was about.

At Stanford it was instituted by that wonderful idiot savant John Hawkes who is a great writer, who at the same time knows absolutely nothing but his wonderful, innocent ideas, and it was his idea that you could make a great writer out of anyone. All you had to do was to find his or her individual voice. So we were all transported across the country by grant or whatever, to Stanford where he directed this project, where we were going to find 150 masterpieces so long as we could take any eight- or nine-year-old kid and find out what the music of his voice was. I'm sure we found no masterpieces at all, but I think he was right to feel that you had to equate the spoken voice with the written voice on the page, even if it was the exact opposite; somehow there had to be a profound relationship between the way people spoke and what was found on the page. What we did was to take young writers and have them talk into a machine, and we went over to East Palo Alto, wherever it was, like an octopus who went everywhere, finding six- and seven-year-old kids, hearing them speak and trying to see if we could emulate the voice or recapture the voice, and I think there was a profundity in it, in that if we *could* capture that voice, we would find something. Well, after months of turmoil and very, very hard work I assure you we came up with nothing!

You can't define voice. It's too idiosyncratic; it's a kind of print, a kind of identifying mark that consists of so many things and so many histories that it's bewildering and yet it's there, one can define Faulkner's voice.

I would give you my definition: it's music, it's music alive with extreme sympathy so that when you read a work by Faulkner, there is no space between you and the text. He adores every one of the characters he writes about—they can be the worst scoundrels—and no other writer other than perhaps Melville or Barthelme has that quality. So we can't simply say that it's language, we can't simply say that it's this unique use of language. It's language *plus*, and it's that plus, that infinity that makes it particularly *you*, so it's something plus something else and that's what is so difficult. Please argue, because there's no reason why you should agree with this. It's a nonsensical theory but I think it works!

Pierre Gault: Our work as critics, then, should be a gesture of recognition, simply? Just to recognize the presence of the voice and try to define it, that's all, but without any set phrase or any set way of describing it, just the gesture?
JC: Yes.

Noëlle Batt: What you say is not true because if it was as easy as that we should simply record you now, put it on the page, and there would be a new book of Jerome Charyn, and you know it's not true!

JC: No, I said it's not true! But what is true is that I'm only speaking for myself. Hearing William Gass read, when I went back to the text somehow I read it in a very different way. I found the rhythm just by listening to his voice.

Marc Chénetier: Counterexample: at least several witnesses are here. Reading John Hawkes. You read John Hawkes and you have this extraordinary voice coming over; then you talk with John Hawkes and you can't read for two years! The opposite applies, you can actually have helping voices over in your head and you can also have debilitating voices!
JC: Okay, but this is not a good example because John Hawkes is the most unconscious writer you can ever find. Just ask him to speak about his own work and what he says about his own work bears no relationship whatsoever to it! So that in one sense he's not a very helpful accomplice. To hear him read is to destroy the text rather than to move closer to it; but that also suggests a kind of schizophrenia in the voice which makes his best works incomparable, it's the schizophrenia. You don't know where you are, you begin *The Lime Twig*, you're here and then suddenly you're in some other place, in some other landscape. It's like working with Krazy Kat. You're in one panel, then the panel changes and suddenly you don't know where you are, with his very best work. You can find some kind of cohabitation in terms of the writer and the text and the music that the text provides; the music may not even be in the author's voice or you may have a superb reader like Stanley Elkin and it may defuse the text as you're reading it. But it seems to me that it's not Stanley reading his text that interests me, it's talking to him when he's not being literary and then getting that voice down as you read the book; that, to me, was incredibly helpful, and not the way he read, which was perfect.

So it's very elusive, it's very difficult but necessary, because *if you don't find the voice in a text*, it becomes completely random and very often you notice—I would say for myself, I pick up a text, I read a paragraph and I don't understand a word, and I don't know what's happening. What's happening is that the music is incoherent for me. They're just words on a page. I can't find the rhythm and therefore I have to stop reading, it's meaningless, it's gibberish; not because it doesn't have a meaning on the page but because that undersong, that underlying music just isn't there.

Marc Chénetier: When you take predetermined structures for your books, say a detective story or a fable like *Pinocchio* or anything else, what is it that you do to it or what is it that you want to do to it that's going to (select one) add/transform/none of the above?

JC: It's always to sabotage the form, to push it to its limits, to play with it and yet make it moving at the same time; it is the best parody, it seems to me, always those parodies that touch you or move you in some way, and you get outside the form that "barks," the form that as you say is a house and you destroy the house at the same time and yet as you're destroying it you're also rebuilding another one, at the same time; you're finding a bigger house than the house that was given. So when it's a baseball novel, it's always the idea of moving outside for me. For example people would say: "You can only write a baseball novel about one season, you need the grammar of a season . . . ," you know at the beginning the hitter will arrive, it doesn't matter what the book is, it always ends up in a kind of World Series. Well, then you throw that away and you write a baseball novel about a left-handed third baseman, which is impossible; not only that, you write a baseball novel about a white player who plays in the Negro League. In other words, you just take all of recorded history, twist it around, and restructure your own myth, to your own liking, everything is possible. It's the same thing, like mythopsychosis. Once you start mythologizing, it never ends, and what is the ending of a text? And where does the text really end? There's a kind of violence in every beginning and there's a similar violence, it's much more violent to end. All of a sudden you're sort of moving, shifting into a page, and then you're getting out of the page, which is frightening to me. But I think it doesn't really end, I think that it continues in an invisible way, an invisible ink, the text becomes a kind of infinity that goes on. It can't stop. It's that disease of mythopsychosis; it doesn't really end. You have the illusion of ending because otherwise the reader would go as mad as *you* are, so you give him a break by saying: "Yes, this is the end!"

Elaine Safer: Voice and style are very closely allied. But there's still a difference. I find a difference between the voice in *Vineland* and the voice in *Gravity's Rainbow* and *V.* Do you?

JC: Yes. But let's go back to that first question: What is the difference between voice and style? Style is something that is much more conscious: it's the writer who's honing images, reworking the sentences, finding a text, that's the style. The voice is something that's much more basic, much more primitive, that underlies the signature of the style, and yet it's something that doesn't change so much from book to book. I think what changes in Pynchon is the style. It's first of all the genius, the absolute genius of parody. He's the greatest parodist probably we've ever had, in that he can do anything. On the one hand, I think that as he creates, he also destroys. Now, in *Vineland*, it's Pynchon twenty years later, it's a different kind of persona. Maybe there's more resignation, maybe there's more sadness. It's playful, but playful with a kind of vengeance. It's a celebration of the end of America, or the end of the possibility of America, but I may be wrong, it's difficult to say. But still, to describe Pynchon's voice would be a very, very difficult thing. If you ask *me*, I would say it's the absence of a voice, it's the writer moving towards invisibility as he assumes one mask after the other and the masks are infinite. He can play with anything as he plays with names, an extraordinary use of names, probably as profound or even more profound than Dickens, the ability to find the right name, and the permutations.

The other thing in Pynchon which is so extraordinary is that you're left with nothing. You end up in a kind of quicksand, everything he creates he destroys one page later so there's no sense of character. The characters are simply fabulations and he plays with, he picks up, throws them away at the same time, from text to text and they don't really change, they're mask upon mask upon mask.

The two texts that I celebrate as a writer, texts that destroyed me, were the early stories of Barthelme and *V.* I had never encountered a book like *V*, because after he creates something in an extraordinary chapter and you say he can't really do anything better than that, the next chapter takes you one stage further, the next chapter even goes beyond that as he tries to define the sensibility of V, so that by the end of the book you're almost strangled in the text. It's an endless kind of weaving. I think for most writers it was *the* revelation of those years, but to define the voice in *V* is extremely difficult. I would almost say it's man hiding behind man. It's brilliant, there's nothing that escapes him, there's nothing he can't write about, he's limitless, he can mythologize and it's not mythopsychosis because I don't think it's a disease, I think he's in absolute control of everything he's doing; but I can't find the voice, I can find the mask but I can't find the voice. This is not a criticism. I'm just saying that what was to me so profound is that it was utterly, absolutely nihilistic. When you end that book, you're left with nothing. There's nothing, because he fabulates and then he destroys the fabulation. He creates V, you say, "Ok, V is here," then in the next chapter V is someplace else, and it's very sad. I was in love with *V*, it's a masterpiece, it's wonderful and beautiful at the same time, and harrowing, an absolute harrowing text.

Pierre Gault: How would you place Nabokov?

JC: In my opinion, the three great American writers are Melville, Faulkner, and Nabokov. All three had an absolute sense of music; if you take the novels that Nabokov wrote in America, a sum of three books: *Pale Fire*, *Pnin*, and *Lolita*, the three variations on the same theme . . . it's difficult to describe, but again, when I read the opening of *Lolita*, the way he describes Lolita's name, I was just overwhelmed; it's incredible, it's the absolute sense of music, it's the sadness. Again I think there is a relationship between *Lolita* and *V*. They're both about this butterfly hunt in which you're left with nothing, except the kind of grace of language and if you go back to Melville, when you look at *Pierre*, what is *Pierre* about, what is *The Confidence Man* about? You're left with nothing. That writer who takes you to the edge, takes you to the precipice, and I think that Hawkes does that too. There's the thing that I love, there's no escape, there's romance but there's no escape, because after all *Lolita* is a love story.

Noëlle Batt: When you say that the voice doesn't change from book to book, what is the implication of that? We tend to conclude that the voice has something to do with the author more than with the text?

JC: Yes, in other words, the voice of the narrator is a kind of impersonation, but the voice of the author is beyond the impersonation. It's the undersong, it's much more basic than the narration because the narration can always change; for example in my own stuff, I would say that it wasn't until a very crazy book called *Eisenhower, My Eisenhower* that I really discovered my own voice, which has nothing to do with the first-person narrator speaking in that text. It was the ability to let go, it was the ability to say "the hell with it!" I don't have to be logical, I don't have to be sane, I don't have to find any order, I can just let the text take care of itself.

And a very real influence was *Second Skin*, the work of John Hawkes. Just to see how far he was able to go, of course not when you spoke to him, you had a completely different person then, someone controlled. This is the old Jack Hawkes, he looked like the mad doctor from Captain Marvel, he had no ears whatsoever, he had these enormous spectacles, and he just was crazed and wonderful. I remember Hawkes said that he had met with a convict at San Quentin who was his greatest reader, because he had read all his books, and when Hawkes went to visit him, the convict said: "Be careful, you're getting a bit soft in your writing!"

Noëlle Batt: And you think that the voice of the author has a fight with the voice of the narrator, somehow?

JC: Yes, I think it is a fight, not a conscious one. I don't think the voice is conscious; the narration is conscious, it's technique, it's building up word upon word, image upon image. The voice isn't conscious, it's a kind of shriek, it's a kind of scream, it's much more primal. You've all seen work that was wonderful, and then from book to book it's not so wonderful and you wonder why. You say the writer is tired, the energy is gone, the ability to create—it's not true! But the voice is strangled, it's hiding, afraid to come out; it could be manic, it could be the opposite, it doesn't really matter.

For example, let's look at Faulkner. If you look at the first two novels, they're absolutely dreadful! They're just imitations of Hemingway, and suddenly you find the voice and from book to book that voice coheres in an extraordinary way and then he loses it again. It becomes pretentious, it becomes silly, it becomes exaggerated, and it never comes back. I think that's true, in a sense you find your rhythm, there's a kind of joy in discovering your rhythm and it will go from text to text and then at some time it will betray you and you'll lose it. I think it's invariably the case. I don't think you can find any exception.

Marc Chénetier: How do you go about the first pages of your books? Do you have an oriented vision of where you're going?

JC: No, I'm terrified, I'm terrified and then I stall. And I write the first sentence and it's no good, and I can't go beyond and it takes me about three weeks to find that first sentence, to take me into the text and after that I'm not afraid.

I find the music, it somehow sounds right. I find the music, and then I say, OK, I'm in the text and I let the dream take over. It doesn't mean I don't revise. I revise a great deal, but I'm not afraid, that's the crucial thing. But to get that first sentence is terrifying. I'm not afraid of ending it, I'm not afraid of doing anything about ending the text, but to start it is a kind of nightmare.

Marc Chénetier: That Barthelme story, "The Dolt": "Middles and ends are OK but to begin, to begin, to begin . . . !"

JC: Exactly. And also, if you look at Barthelme, there's a curious contradiction. He's the great story writer trying to be a novelist, and what makes him a great story writer means that he can't be a novelist, and that he can never reconcile it throughout his entire life. He was sad and depressed that he wasn't a Dostoievskian novelist. And he just didn't understand that the talent he had, the extraordinary ability to telescope within two or three or five pages an entire narrative, was the very thing that made it impossible for him to be a novelist though he has written novels and they're good novels, but they're not great ones. And the stories *are* great, they're incomparable, and he could never reconcile one with the other.

Now some people might say that to begin is very easy, you just start and you change it and put it on the computer and let the computer write it and then you can just go on. But I don't find that. I find that when I have the rhythm I have the text. As a matter of fact, I know it will sound silly to say that but, as I'm writing one book, I'm dreaming the next. By the time I finish the book, I've already in my own head sort of written the next one. I'm not even aware of it. If you ask me what the book is about, if you asked me who the characters are, I don't know! But somehow it's there, it's the dreamscape, the dreamwalking, that's where the rhythm comes from, and that's where the voice is when it gets blocked. It's the writer who can no longer dream, and therefore can't find the sense of music, even though the basic talent is there!

Noëlle Batt: Since you're writing with music, when you read other writers, you try to get their music. Do you ever find interferences between your music and that of other writers?

JC: No, there's never any interference. As a matter of fact, when you read a writer, let's say when I discovered Barthelme and saw that I would never write sentences the way he could write a sentence, it didn't threaten me. It almost made me feel that there was something I could learn and this is the real education, so it's never threatening to find writers that are great; it may destroy you in terms of your wanting to absorb it and internalize it, but I think you need to hear the music of other writers. When I first began writing stories, I happened to stumble upon "The Pedersen Kid," and in a way it changed my life! It's an extraordinary text, it's incomparable. I don't know how to describe it—the text about the disappearance of the American psyche. The fact that I knew that I could never write a text as good as that didn't make me sad because in some way I was able to incorporate it in my own head, it became mine. I don't mean I stole from it but I absorbed it, I learned from it, and therefore in my own small way I could use it as I could also use John Hawkes. I had no music at that point; I had written six novels where I simply impersonated six voices, six first-person voices. Then I went to California, where I had somehow unconsciously found a voice that was mine. I don't say it was good. It was *Eisenhower, My Eisenhower*; it's an incomprehensible book but it doesn't matter! As a matter of fact, that's the book Pynchon really loved; he said: "That book is crazier than mine!"

Noëlle Batt: And then you kept it?
JC: Kept the voice? No, it's not that I kept it, I wasn't doing impersonations any more. In other words, until that point I was really faking. I could get into a voice academically, I could research it, I could write it, but it was really an impersonation. After that, good or bad, it was not an impersonation any more. Now most writers by six failures would have stopped! Finally, what was working was that something internal was happening; each of the texts was a kind of waltz, a kind of dance. It doesn't mean that I might not have lost that music or voice, but it's at that point that I didn't usurp, that I could really feel I was writing my own text.

Again, I can't speak for anyone else. Maybe you dream of an ideal reader but I think you are your own ideal reader, you are the composer. I hate to get into psychology, but it's very true! We cannot pretend to be continuous people. For example, I'm about to write a page. If I write it today it will be one thing; if I write it tomorrow it will be a completely different page. Therefore when I assemble 250 pages, how do I dare call it a novel? How do I dare pretend that it has a continuous line when it really doesn't? But the 3,018 sentences, 217,000 words strung together under the illusion of what one calls the novel, and I don't think that's the case, I don't think that's true. I think publishers have to pretend they've given you a text that coheres, but I would say that the very best texts don't cohere at all; and that's what makes them extraordinary, that they're flirting with a kind of anarchy; this is what makes them powerful: the ability to just move to the very edge, to maybe go over, and I think maybe that's what the wise convict was saying to John Hawkes, when he said: "You've gone to the wall, step back a little bit because you're going to fall and fall very far!"

Marc Chénetier: We've reached the point where we confirm the idea that "you ain't got a thing if you ain't got the swing!"

Elaine Safer: You put your finger on something I was looking forward to finding here. That voice is actually nonliterary, it is everything that is nonliterary, and it is something that comes from pulsion, from the unconscious. It is the presence of the pulsion and its breath in the text and that's why it is so hard for us to say where it is and how you can pin it down. When it's carried through a text, it becomes very difficult to separate, to abstract it from the words.

JC: I'm not sure you could abstract it. You could only say that when you take a particular writer and suddenly by the fourth book or the third book something is appearing that was not in the earlier two books, is it the development of craft? I'm not sure! There's a kind of breath in there, it comes alive on the page in a perverse way. Suddenly you're very close to the characters, you're close to the persons and the language and then it may drift off; a novel estranged: fifty pages are working beautifully, the next twenty-five put you to sleep. We expect that because it's a kind of journey. I would say reading is like being on a horse, it's like galloping on a crazy horse. This is the way I would define my own writing—I won't talk about anyone else—but it's really being on a horse, and sometimes the horse falls asleep, and sometimes it goes at a terrific pace and sometimes it dies, it just dies on you!

Marc Chénetier: But still, it's all very well if you define the voice as something that to a certain extent you're listening to yourself but nobody else will listen to say, it's pulsion, it's self-conscious. This being said, ask poor lay people reading a text. They also hear something, it must be there! There is something there and, as Barthelme would put it: "It's not between the lines, it's in the 'bloody lines,' it's there!" So I'm still sorry to be so positivistic about all this, but it must be somewhere where we feel it!

JC: You misunderstood me! I said that when I read a text, I hear the voice too, but of course you're hearing the voice of the writer. What is that voice that you're hearing, and why is the voice suddenly more powerful in one instance and less powerful in another instance? That's difficult to define! Is it the breakdown of language? I think it's a kind of rhythm that may cohere around a character, that may cohere around a scene, when suddenly something is ignited, something comes alive, something is made personal. I would say the voice can only be personal, it can't be impersonal. It's a very specific signature.

When you talk about Faulkner's language, there is something else there that's so primitive, that's so powerful, that draws you just into the characters, into the psyche. There's no distance between you and the page, and at that point the voice is ultimate, the voice takes over. As you go, let's say in *The Sound and the Fury*, from Benjy to Jason, there's something that just moves you in an extraordinary way; you could say it's technique, four different points of view, but there are millions of novels with four different points of view! Anybody could have come upon that idea, but it's the ability to just take you *into* the text, and that's difficult to talk about.

For example, what is "The Pedersen Kid" about? It's about nothing. It's about a kid who may or may not have been in the snow. Does the kid exist? Nobody is sure. Has there been a kind of murder? Maybe, maybe not. Maybe nothing happened! It's about snow, it's about whiteness, and he's lying between the whiteness. That's it! So I don't know—we could talk about, we could articulate it but would we ever really find it?

You can't imitate the voice, because the voice is a kind of print that is unique. You could imitate the trappings of the voice but never the voice. I don't think so.

"Chanting in the Dark": An Interview with Jerome Charyn

Gilles Menegaldo / 1995

This interview took place on November 18, 1995, at the University of Poitiers and was never published. Printed by permission of Gilles Menegaldo.

GM: Good morning Jerome, and thank you for accepting this interview. The first question could be: how did you come to writing? Could you speak a little of your background, your relations to books, for instance, and more generally to language and culture?

JC: Well, I had no language and culture; that was the real problem. I grew up in a very poor area of the South Bronx, my parents barely spoke English, and so it was very difficult for me to discover language. I discovered images before language. I was an artist. I began to draw, but I really saw drawings in a very peculiar way, as stories. So it was very natural to move from images into words, because I felt that words also had images. And for me, to deal with language was almost a question of life and death, because I had to find some way of learning it if I was going to survive, and it didn't seem to happen in school. I had, for example, hysterical problems about hearing—at first the people in school thought I was deaf because I just couldn't concentrate, I couldn't learn, I couldn't listen. So I had all these hearing tests, you know, with sounds and bells coming into your ears, and I discovered that I had no hearing problems at all. So what I began to discover is that if I saw words as images, if I saw them in my mind, I could learn them. And therefore I began to write as if I were drawing and I began to draw as if I were writing—that's the curious paradox. So, for me, there's always been a profound relationship between images and words, and that's one reason why I moved into the graphic novel of *bande dessinée*, and also into illustrated texts.

GM: What about culture? Did you have any discovery that led you, that urged you to write?

JC: As I said, writing was really a means of soothing myself. I had nothing to do with culture, because I had no sense of culture. It's only when I went to the university, for example, that I really began to read, and I began to discover that there was a world, a systematic world of books and ideas, and so for me the first years at the university were really a revelation. I mean, I didn't know that Franz Kafka existed, so when I began to read *The Castle* and *The Trial*, I saw that there was a paradigm for my own existence, that my own feeling of guilt—now, I'd found a resource to rediscover what my own feeling of guilt was about, and it was the feeling of guilt about being alive, and suddenly it was in these texts, in these very marvelous texts by Dostoevsky, by Kafka, or by Tolstoy. So reading became a necessary act, a reflexive act. I began to read everything. All I needed from the university was a reading list. And once my professors gave me that reading list, I could practically do it on my own. And my interpretations of texts were always different from my teachers', as I saw them in a very different way.

GM: Could you give me examples of that?

JC: For example, when I read Sophocles, for instance the story of Philoctetes and the magical bow—yes, it's true that it can be seen as a reference for art, but it's also again about guilt, about having sinned and really having no way to redeem oneself in relation to that sin. So I began to see books as having certain symbolic frames, certain symbolic meanings that were really outside the literal rendering of the text itself. And I was in a class, a sort of brainchild class for those students who were studying literature. One of the students is now a Nobel Prize winner, one or the other is a director, whatever it is, and we would give our teachers a nervous breakdown because they could never keep up with our own rendering of the texts. These were very curious kids from the Bronx in Manhattan, who were not trained traditionally but really looked at these texts in a very raw, personal way. So I wasn't unique in this. But as we read texts as a question of life and death and we devoured them in a very particular way, we really puzzled our teachers, because they were giving us traditional textbook renderings of Dostoeysky or Molière or whatever it was, and we had already gone beyond that.

GM: I think in one interview you said you considered yourself at that time as a golem. Could you comment on that, because a golem, of course, is part of the Jewish tradition.

JC: Yes, but it's a golem in that I really grew up without a culture, without a sense of the past, and I was a golem who was learning, discovering language for the first time, and I felt like a kind of monster in relation to language. But on the other hand I was lucky enough, very, very fortunate enough to master words, because that was the only equipment I really had. I had no practical equipment—even coming out of my hotel, today, I couldn't open the door, I was locked in my hotel room, I twisted left, twisted right and the door didn't open. I couldn't make the television set work yesterday, I couldn't close the shower, I couldn't make the water go off. So what I experience daily is a sort of an everyday disassociation with the planet around me, and it was only through words, through trying to master them, in a very difficult way because it took me years and years, that I felt a kind of confidence, that the only thing in the world that I could do, was really to have a magical relation with words. So words still remain magical to me, so I'm a golem. I'm the monster, with no one to save except myself.

GM: To speak about the beginning of your career now. You wrote quite a number of novels prior to the initiating of the Isaac Sidel cycle. Could you tell us about these first books, which so far are very hard to find?
JC: *Once upon a Droshky* was my first attempt, but let's not use the word career, because I don't think the word career really is what one's life is about. It's an adventure in trying to write, and fortunately or unfortunately one has to live, so one has to earn a living, and that's the sole relationship with careers, that is an exchange of money. The first novel that I wrote is called *Once upon a Droshky*, and it's about an old Yiddish actor on the Lower East Side, who's been locked out of his profession and locked out of his apartment house, and basically he lives in a cafeteria and the book is about his adventures in the cafeteria in relation to his language as an actor.

GM: You also say that *Eisenhower, My Eisenhower* is one of the first books in which you actually found experimental language?
JC: I found my music. I can't say experimental language, but with the earlier books I really felt I was using a kind of literary language that I had learnt or studied in school and I was trying to copy or emulate this kind of language. With *Eisenhower, My Eisenhower*, I felt that I'd found out my own mythology and the music to deal with that mythology. *Eisenhower, My Eisenhower* is about a group of gypsies who have tails, and they fornicate with their tails, so they can literally fuck themselves, and in a way, everyone is opposed to these gypsies, you know, everyone hates them because they have this kind

of sexual power. It's a novel of the late sixties or early seventies about all the madness that was going on in the United States—Vietnam, the ghettoes, the explosion in the ghettoes, and these gypsies are everyone's target, you know, because they have this magical power.

GM: The Sidel saga, which now counts nine titles, has become central to your work. Could you speak of its genesis? How did the idea first come to you?

JC: It really began because my brother is a policeman, and it was in examining the sadness of his own life that I came to the notion of writing crime novels—I wouldn't have been able to do it otherwise. It was his intelligence, the sadness of being in a world that was so limiting, a world where he had nowhere to go, basically, as a policeman, and all he could do was deal with violence, and he became violent in relation to this violence. And seeing him as a sort of soft killer inspired me to write about Manfred Coen and to see Isaac Sidel as his keeper, as his puppeteer in a way, and then, once Coen dies in the middle of the ending of the book, it then becomes Isaac Sidel's remembering of Coen and his haunting by Coen that inspire the later books. But they're not really crime novels. They're novels about criminals and policemen, but they contain the same literary games; I play the same literary games that I do in my other novels.

GM: Could you speak of the character of Sidel—has it got certain models in reality or have you been influenced by specific writers or texts?

JC: Well, the character changed. In the first four books, he goes from being a peripheral character to being the central character in *Secret Isaac*, and in a way the real influence for all those books was James Joyce, and the music of James Joyce, and also Faulkner—doing a kind of Faulknerian landscape in the city of New York, my own Yoknapatawpha County. But after the first four books, I turned to other things, and it was only when I was writing *Metropolis*, which is a sort of historical, personal study of New York City, it was after going around with Mayor Koch, and seeing *him* as a fictive event *[laughs]*, a kind of gangster, I mean, a wonderful gangster, who's more powerful than those sources around him, which is one reason I admire him—he was frightened by no one. He was really the King of New York, and he ran it the way he wanted to run it. That's when I became further involved with the idea of Isaac Sidel, and Sidel suddenly becomes the Mayor of New York. So it was by reinvestigating New York City in *Metropolis* that I decided to go back to the *Saga* and to sort of transform it into something else.

GM: What is your own private relation with that character?

JC: I think I had myself moved closer to being that character. At first, Isaac was a sort of evil father figure, then he became a kind of brother, and as he grew older and I grew older with him . . . I wouldn't say he became an *alter ego*, I wouldn't say a double, but he cannibalized me and I cannibalized him and at some point we came together.

GM: Would you consider—since you talked about guilt a moment ago—that one of the central metaphors in the series is that of the worm . . .

JC: Yes.

GM: . . . that is gnawing the interiors of Sidel. Why did you emphasize that metaphor in various novels, and how did the meaning of it change?

JC: Well, you could call the worm his conscience. That's a little bit too easy. The worm is his interior voice, you know. He eats for the worm to survive and the worm eats him at the same time, but it's a kind of corrective for Isaac. It's his ability to talk to himself, to find a spokesman who will challenge him and not betray him—because the worm never really betrays him. Sidel may betray the worm, but the worm will cannibalize him without ever betraying him. And I also love this idea of this tapeworm that one couldn't get rid of and that Isaac had to sort of drink bottles of milk to feed it, but of course in the later books, he is shot and the worm dies as Isaac recovers. So when Isaac no longer has the worm, he no longer has this interior music and as he rises further and further into the hierarchy of being the first Deputy Commissioner, of being a Police Commissioner and then Mayor of New York, he becomes more and more isolated, more and more alone.

GM: Do you mean that he loses part of his humanity while he succeeds in his career?

JC: No, he doesn't lose part of his humanity, it's just that he loses that soft relationship with himself. He's still very much involved with the disruption and the chaos around him, but he has no center to deal with that corruption.

GM: Yes, because what is fairly different in the case of Sidel from other famous detective characters is the way he loves finding his enemies, in a way . . .

JC: Yes.

GM: . . . and he mingles with them, becomes part of the Mafia at one point, but at the same time he keeps a kind of personal moral all the time. Could you elucidate that apparent paradox? Sidel is going against the law, in many ways, he's also a criminal.

JC: In order to follow the law, one has to go against the law. This is the contradiction of New York City, which is chaotic and lawless, so in order to bring back the law, he has to become part of the chaos. When one of his associates, Sweets, who becomes the Commissioner, replaces him, he says to Isaac, "Isaac, you always has to go inside the elephant's ass." And this is indeed what he has to do. He has to sort of crawl into the heart of darkness in order to deal with the darkness. One of my favorite works is Joseph Conrad's *Heart of Darkness*, and I think there are always references to that particular text in mine.

GM: Maybe we'll come back to this notion of quest later on, but to return for a moment to the question of genre. Obviously, as has been repeatedly said, your books are not classical crime fictions.

JC: No.

GM: They are various modes of subversions of the genre. You play with the rules and with the expectations of the reader as well—you baffle the expectations of the reader in a way. For instance, could you tell us about this complexity of plot and narrative, and the incredible imagination you develop in these stories in which the reader gets lost in a maze of plots and subplots?

JC: Out of necessity I believe in the exploding text, that is the text that not only twists and turns around, but literally explodes and creates its own twin, so that there are the text and the undertext, or the undersong, at the same time and the dialogue is between those texts that keep varying. It's a kind of constant permutation. So that, yes, it's probably difficult for the reader to follow, but at the same time if you lend yourself to the text, I think it takes you much further. I mean, I always see the novel as a kind of exploration, a kind of adventure into the darkness or into another planet, and either you let yourself go and swim in this crazy world, or you resist it and you give up reading. But this is where I have to go in order to write. It's the only kind of text that really makes sense to me and it's the only kind of text that I myself can enter into. So that there is no safe ground—characters can change, their personalities can change, all the characters are aspects of the same character or aspects of the same voice, and therefore you have to put this music together in order to survive in the text, so that the actual act of reading becomes a matter of life and death, it seems to me. There has to be a tremendous investment in order to survive the text, and probably not many readers can do that, but on the other hand, this is what I want to do, this is what I need to do, and this is what I do.

GM: The central notion of investigation is also subverted. The investigation becomes peripheral in a way. And what is more important indeed is that notion of quest.
JC: Yes.

GM: Perhaps you could define that notion. There's also the idea of spatial exploration, which usually implies displacement in various ways. Also sometimes a quest that doesn't seem that important becomes essential whereas there is no apparent reason for that. I'm thinking of *Secret Isaac*, when Sidel goes to Ireland to inquire about the girl, and there is this Joycean intertext. Why this quest?
JC: The question is really the attempt to discover who *you* are in relation to those people around you. But the thing is, what do you really learn about yourself as you enter the hall of mirrors? I like *The Lady from Shangai*, the Orson Welles film that ends with the image where you literally cannot find who you are in relation to these mirrors, and it seems to me that this is what the quest is all about: how do you get to the other side of these mirrors, and the answer is that you can't, but you always have to try. And this is the position that I feel I am in. I mean, how can I discover who I am in relation to the child that I was and the child that I've remained and the child that I'll always be? I don't mean this in a sentimental way, but as I learnt English so late, I'm always a child in relation to language. You master it in some sense but it always escapes you. The more you master it, it seems to me, the less you know. So the more vocabulary you acquire, the more words you forget at the same time. And this is what the quest is about—it's trying to find your own outline in the world that's out there, and the realization that you'll never get this outline. But you may have fun along the way; I mean that's the important thing. If you look at the dialogue, which often seems irrelevant, it's not irrelevant because something is trying to be discovered underneath this kind of constant jabber, the attempt to find a line or thread in this sort of chaotic kind of landscape, so that you can walk along the line and find your way in this very strange maze.

GM: Since you speak about chaos: chaos is also important in the way your books subvert the traditional crime novels. The function of the detective or the policeman is usually to reestablish order in chaos, whereas not the function but at least the result of these happenings in your novels seems on the contrary to reinforce chaos.

JC: Yes, to add to it, to multiply the chaos. This is the inescapable lesson. Isaac always tries to get beyond the chaos in order to really reestablish order, but the harder he tries, in a way, the more chaos he brings around him. But he still must try, that is his quest, it's to find answers to questions, and the more answers he finds, the more questions he discovers—there are ten times more questions. That's what I mean when I mention Philoctetes and the magical bow that is supposed to solve the problem of the Trojan War. He's the only one who can use the bow, and on the other hand the magical bow, which is, let's say, the bow of language, is always beyond you, always escapes you, so that the more you own this bow, the more you become the master of it, the more it whirls back at you and brings you deeper into the chaos, it seems to me. But there is always a pleasure in using this language, and I think that the deepest pleasure is in the singing, in the music—the bow is a kind of harp.

GM: You were just referring to myth or Greek culture, but you tend to make more and more explicit now, even in terms of words, the relationship between what you try to describe, especially with the background of New York, the big metropolis, and certain laws of contemporary physics. This seems to be an interest that is shared with other writers—I'm thinking of Ian McEwan for instance. Could you explain how it came to be more explicit in your work?

JC: I think that's an unconscious reaction to the disorder around us. We have to find a language to sort of greet this disorder, to deal with it, to come to terms with it. But I think it's the writer or the technician—or whatever you want—really absorbing the atmosphere, the deepest sense of the atmosphere, and trying to find some way to embrace it. For me, the greatest texts are always those texts that come the closest to chaos, as for example *The Sound and the Fury*. I mean, if you pushed ten degrees further, it would be an incomprehensible text. But that's why I love Faulkner so much, because he's found the music within this chaos, and I have to laugh when people talk about him as a Southern writer, as a sort of agrarian writer trying to recapture the great past. It's complete nonsense. The subtext has nothing to do with the texture of the South. It's much more powerful, much more limitless than that. It's the riddle of language that he's trying to solve and can never really solve.

GM: Since you refer to Faulkner, there is another way in which you subvert the crime novel—and this is something you may share with Faulkner: the emphasis on grotesqueness.

JC: Yes.

GM: For instance, one vivid image I keep from the Sidel saga is the description of the Guzman family, and that particular character of Jeronimo, who is a criminal but also a childish, almost helpless figure. You find this again in the Mino brothers and various characters in your work—and the Geek as well is a case in point.

JC: To me another thing that makes Faulkner such a great writer is that he invests his own psyche in every single character. I'm thinking of the Snopes—I mean, they're absolutely hateful, but you adore them. And his sympathies go so far, *so* deep, and the same thing is true for Dostoevsky; that's why I think they're probably two of the greatest writers. In a way, it's beyond technique, I mean their sympathies are so deep that you cannot help but enter these texts and have them completely take you over. I'm thinking of *The Devils* by Dostoevsky, or *The Brothers Karamazov*. You're so involved in these characters and in the world of these characters that they haunt you for life, you never escape them.

GM: What about your own fondness for a character like the Geek or some other grotesques that we find in your books. Even Sidel, in a way, is a grotesque.

JC: But you see, I don't see them as grotesques. I see them as logical extensions of who we all really are. I mean, the fact that we hide our own grotesque nature and want to pretend that we're not grotesque when in some way we really are. So that the Geek, who's someone who's sort of outside the borders of what's possible—a man who feeds on garbage, human garbage—to me is also very touching because he has his own sense of aesthetics, where he wants to survive, needs to survive, has to survive, and will survive.

GM: So in other words, you have a more positive evaluation of grotesqueness, the way Sherwood Anderson does, for instance, in *Winesburg, Ohio*?

JC: Yes, and I was thinking of Sherwood Anderson's story about hands, "Hands." Yes, I think that *Winesburg, Ohio* is a marvelous book; it's a book that I absolutely adore. And maybe it's the first time in American literature that we see this ambivalence about grotesqueness. Of course, it's completely subsumed in Dickens's books, it's all about grotesque and his greatest characters are always grotesques, it seems to me.

GM: There's also Carson McCullers, of course.

JC: Yes, but that's later.

GM: Well, maybe to summarize that reference to the crime novel and to the *roman noir*, how far would you consider your novels as *romans noirs*, both in terms of subject matter and style?

JC: I would see them as *romans noirs* in terms of atmosphere, in terms of nihilism, in terms of the idea of language as amnesia, in terms of the quest that gets you nowhere, in terms of this desire or need to attack the society, not as a preacher but as a singer of songs. To me, the greatest *romans noirs* are those of Dashiell Hammett. In his greatest texts, it seems to me that the *privé* enters the landscape, creates complete disorder, and then moves out of the landscape. I'm thinking particularly of *Red Harvest*, this unnamable detective who really only adds to the crime and is a criminal on the side of the law. And I think really we have to see the police in this way. I don't mean this negatively, but I think that in a lawless world, the police are only part of this lack of law.

GM: If we come now to more formal matters, I've tried to distinguish several styles in your work, but you said that even for each of the Sidel novels, there is a particular style. Could you provide an example for these different styles?

JC: Well, again, there are permutations in the texts. If you look at *Secret Isaac*, it's completely different from *Blue Eyes*, in other words it's much more lyrical, it's much more somber, and yet it has a kind of manic side that the other books don't. So it seems to me that the permutation or the change in style is probably an internal one. It's where *you* are at a particular moment in relation to the text, and also it's about a kind of schizophrenia that we all seem to have in relation to the text. For instance, if you were thinking of writing a page one day and you happened to write the same page the next day, it would be completely different because of the tone or the mood or the situation that you're in. So we think of texts as continuous lines, continuous stories, when they're not. Each sentence exists in its own sort of stratosphere and what connects these sentences is only the reader's desire or need or sense of cohesion or need to cohere, but it seems to me that the texts themselves are completely chaotic.

GM: One aspect that impressed me a lot in *Secret Isaac* is that expedition of Dermot and Annie the girl, when they climb the mountain—they're supposed to go on a picnic?

JC: Well, this was an event that—I myself, I took Dermot's trip with my own Annie, you know. I was on that trip, so it had its own . . . I was on Cashel Hill, so again I was Dermot at that particular moment, I was the gangster that could hire his own restaurant, who could collect Faulkner—I mean this kind of crazy *mélange*. I don't mean the gangster in a romantic way. I mean that person who exists on the side of the law as a kind of necessity. And I think the writer *is* a gangster. The writer *must* exist on the side of the culture, of the law, in order to reinterpret it, in order to attack it, in order to embrace it. So the notion of gangster-writer is very, very important to me. All writers, in some way, are criminals, because they take, they steal from the language—you know, the words are there for you to steal, you don't own them, you know, you have to steal them.

GM: Yes, well, I felt something very authentic in that account and at the same time something very poetic—I mean that account of the mountain trip. But at the same time, it was also fairly violent, and this leads me to another aspect, another thing that you seem to emphasize and consider as essential. It's the violence of language—not only the violence of events, which is obvious in your books (there are crimes etc.), but also the way in which language itself becomes a weapon.

JC: But it's so cruel. I mean language itself is without mercy and the thing I hate most is the idea of sentimentality, which to me is false language. I mean, you can have sentiment, you can have a great deal of feeling, but to me sentimentality is the over-response to feeling. It's the other side of feeling; it's the false side of feeling. But if you think about language, it's a kind of sword that you use to create motion and to destroy things, to attack things. I think language itself is barbaric, or it has become barbaric, or, as Roland Barthes says in *Writing Degree Zero*, for the modern writer "language exists outside of history in menace," it has become the instrument of menace. So that, in a way, all writing may very well be crime writing.

GM: I think you said in one of your interviews that language is devoid of sentiment.

JC: No, no, I say that false language is an over-response to sentiment, it moves into sentimentality, it's soft language, it's language filled with fat.

GM: Another interesting thing is the emphasis you lay upon the notion of blank space between the sentences. That's a very Conradian metaphor, the fact that the meaning is not in the center, but it is on the periphery. You speak of the notion of blank space between the sentences, where you consider that meaning resides, which postulates a certain relationship with the reader.

JC: Yes. It forces the reader to enter into the text, to enter into these white spaces and to really become a co-creator. It is, I think, one of the things that the best modern writing is about, this growing distance between the sentences, so that each sentence becomes a kind of perverse, isolated island. And it's only the reader who can finally make the connections, it's the reader who has to enter into the landscape and use his or her own imagination for the story to make any kind of sense.

GM: Do you think this is connected with a different way of using syntax, for instance?

JC: Yes, I think the modern syntax has changed radically—that's why I say that language has become cruel—because connectives are no longer used. In other words the sentences have become shorter, and they've become more and more startling in terms of things that have been left out rather than are put in. But one of the predicaments is that with the growing use of the computer, of writing on computers, language is again becoming verbose, texts are becoming longer and longer, and we're losing this sense of rapier, we're losing this sword. I think one survey has demonstrated that works of fiction or nonfiction have been 20 percent longer since this obsessive use of the computer.

GM: A good example could be Stephen King. He is the product of that computer age. He writes very huge novels.

JC: Well, I would not want to disparage Stephen King. I think it's a more general problem. Maybe we're losing this edge as we move onto the screen. Something is being lost, I really feel that. And it's inevitable, it's going to be with us, so we're going to have more and more of these connectives, and we're going to have more and more padded language, which to me is the enemy of good writing.

GM: Your own language is rather clipped and your sentences are short, especially in your latest books. For instance, in *Montezuma's Man*, I was struck by the shortness of the sentences, by a kind of editing of syntax.

JC: I think it's the music that I'm hearing. You know, in a way, one hopes to evolve, one hopes to change, one hopes to—let's not even say to grow but to multiply in some sense. This is an unconscious movement, and it seems to me that where I want to go now is not towards multiplicity, it's towards the singular, towards the isolated movement, and so the texts are becoming probably shorter and shorter.

GM: Repetition also seems to be a key notion in your work. For instance thematic repetition, which may be connected with the notion of obsession. For instance the character of Coen: of course, he is killed, but he reappears in various ways, first through the testimonies of several characters, but also in other characters that are doubles of him—Patrick Silver or Joe Barbarossa in the latest one, in which he constantly has to say: "I'm not Blue Eyes, I'm not Coen." Could you tell me about this thematic repetition?

JC: I think it goes beyond themes, it's a kind of echolalia, it's the child hearing words and repeating them in an obsessive way. And it's my hysterical desire to repeat: in order to own the words, you have to magically repeat them. This echolalia is very pronounced in Harold Pinter. Pinter is really one of my great inspirations. *The Homecoming* to me is such an extraordinary text, because it's about families and the breakdown of families and it's the interior world of the way people speak to each other, the kind of hostility that most people have to most familial situations. So I think the doubling or tripling of Coen and the multiplication of Coen goes back to Isaac's obsessive guilt, to having killed Coen, but beyond that Coen simply refuses to die. So he's reborn as the writer looks for so many rebirths. Each text is also about a kind of death: as you progress into a text, language dies, and then it has to be born again. That's why sequels are so crazy, they're almost false rebirths, but they're not really rebirths.

GM: I didn't mean it was only thematic. I was coming to the lexical and syntactic side. Because the thematic is, let's say, emphasized by the lexical and the rhetoric of repetition.

JC: The thing is that, again, when we talk about theme, is theme locked up in the music of language, is theme only a kind of afterthought to the music, is theme just the hysterical desire or the need of the reader to find some kind of meaning inside the music? So I'm very suspicious of the word theme.

GM: Yes, I'm suspicious too. But for instance, we could speak of the theme of the father and son, which echoes the relation between Sidel and his various son-figures.

JC: But then you can say that all fathers are their own sons at the same time, it's a multiplication of fathers and sons. Just as language multiplies and re-echoes in this kind of echolalia, so children multiply in relation to their own fathers. What is the Guzman family? It's a kind of phantom-like multiplication of voices.

GM: Is it a way to avoid the actual traumatic problem of the relation between father and son?

JC: I think it is, but also I think the deepest desire for me in any text is to give pleasure. In other words, if I can smile and consider myself the reader, if the reading can produce a smile, but a smile in the deepest sense, you know, if the text, through all its terror, can make you feel happy, can complete you in some way, then I think the text is successful, even though it's disruptive and frightening. That's why really, in the midst of all this chaos, I insist on a happy ending, and people say: "What do you mean? These texts are so dark, so black, and yet it all seems to come together. Why? I mean, it should destroy you, it should disintegrate." But beyond the disintegration, there is a final kind of order. So that if you look at almost all the books, there's always a happy ending. *[Laughs]*

GM: I was struck by the end of *Montezuma's Man*, with the wedding, and the coming together of Margaret Tolstoy and Isaac.

JC: Yes, but it's necessary. It's like being in Disneyland. After I show you the monsters, okay, you want to get out of the car and feel good.

GM: So that would be a way in which you reintroduce a kind of order? Well, I see you smiling when speaking of that, but another important aspect of this work, of course, which sometimes again drifts away from the tradition, is the use of comic elements.

JC: Comic elements, yes, and also it's the exhilaration of music. For example, I'm always happy when I read a page of William Gass. The writing is so musical, so destructive in disassociations that I always have to smile. And there aren't many writers who can make me smile. And I think it's the pleasure of the text, moving through a text, to me that's the deepest pleasure. And certainly it's in every page of *Heart of Darkness*, this kind of almost lush, vegetable growth of the language itself.

GM: I agree with that metaphor of the vegetable growth, because indeed it's very pregnant in Conrad. But I don't think Conrad is that humorous.

JC: No, Conrad isn't humorous at all, there's very little humor in him, but that text to me is a text about this quest. When you finally get to Kurtz, what do you really discover? After, the journey, after going down the river into the heart of darkness, you discover very little.

GM: There may be a relation to establish between two things we spoke about: on the one hand, obsession-repetition and obsessive repetition, on the other hand, amnesia. These two elements seem to be a kind of driving force of your writing. And as you said, you were more and more interested also in coming back to some kind of past.

JC: You find this combination in a text like William Gass's "The Pedersen Kid." The text is about the search for a so-called missing boy, and then as the search deepens, the language disappears into a kind of wonderful snow-storm, where you really don't know where you are in relation to the characters. What Gass is doing there is really dealing again with the savagery and the sadness and the cruelty of language, which finally gives us a kind of solace as it destroys, and it seems to me what language is about is also the forgetting of language, it's the disintegration of who we are. We're dying from the moment we're born, but at the same time we're also receivers of language, and we're receivers of language who then take what we receive and reinvent it in incredible multiples. You know, I think of the child singing to himself or herself and reinventing the sounds of words. So the real reinvention is in the sound, and the meaning only comes later, but what are you finally left with? It seems to me you're left with sounds, or as Faulkner says you're left with sound and fury, and very little else.

GM: Would you consider that a character like Holden is emblematic of that?

JC: Yes, because Holden again goes back to Holden Caulfield, to Salinger's *The Catcher in the Rye*. He is a man who was trained very early to become a killer, and his persona is in relation to the idea of killing people, but again, it's the writer who also kills people. So that, to me, Holden is a character who has no past, who must live in the present and project himself into the future. And what is his *métier*, what is his expertise? His expertise is destruction, but it's destruction that is very, very creative at the same time. So in a way, I'm very fond of this character, though I couldn't tell you what it really means, I have no idea what it means.

GM: It's also one of the books in which the notion of simulacrum, substitutes, false realities, theatricalities is most prominent.

JC: Well, again, there are false steps. Every step we take is a false step, but these false steps combine into a kind of history, into a kind of story, into a kind of narrative. So if you have enough false steps, you have a novel.

GM: We spoke about some of the writers you admire—Conrad or Joyce, for instance. There's one thing that makes you part of the postmodern movement (although I don't particularly like that word); it's the relation that you establish between your own text and the intertext, the other text. How do you situate yourself in relation to that function of the intertext in literature?

JC: It's very hard to describe. When we think of intertext, I think of the face behind the screen, and the search for that face behind the screen, which is monstrous and frightening, but it is also the outline of our own face. And I think what's happening more and more is that there's a profound interrelationship between words on a page and the screen. It's not simply that films are becoming more novelistic, and that novels are becoming more like films. I think there is a disturbing relationship between words and images that hasn't finally really been explored. But it seems to me that novels are moving onto a kind of screen, with all the ambiguities of what screen suggests.

GM: You are referring to something I wanted to ask you afterwards, your relation with the world of cinema. But to come back to heritage: what is your way of integrating that heritage that you finally found out? You said that at first you had no heritage, but then you had one, and it constantly crops up in your work.

JC: It's the heritage of language, I think; it's finding a past in language. I've always felt that, whatever difficulties I had in writing—and there were times when I was completely paralyzed—words never really betrayed me. It's the only thing in my life that I felt—whatever lack of ability I have, whatever limitations I have—it's still to me—I don't know how to say—deeply *soothing* to write, whatever limits there may be in the writing, and I would have no idea what those limits are. There's a quality of—it's difficult to say. The heritage is not simply in other writers, but it's in other songs. I see texts as songs, as singers singing to soothe themselves: we're all sort of stuck in the same room trying to chant and chanting in the dark, it seems to me.

GM: You said that language never betrayed you. This leads me to one question that could be central, and that could be related to ethics in a way also: the relationship between the false and the true in your work, and especially in your pseudo-autobiographical novels.

JC: Yes. When I saw *Pulp Fiction*, and I had to see it several times to really appreciate it, I felt that here was someone who not so much understood the novel or was influenced by the novel, but was doing novelistic films, compartmentalized films where he was outside of the ordinary *mise en scène* of cinema and was inside a kind of text where characters could appear, reappear, could die, could come back to life, could talk complete jabber, where there was a very strange relationship between the image and the word spoken. I felt that this was an incredible breakthrough in terms of the narrative fiction of the film and the idea of the deep narrative, of the possibilities of narrative that films could suddenly have. I wouldn't say it's as complex as a novel, because that's not doing justice to the film. It's *more* complex than a novel. I saw a kind of unconscious complexity and I saw a kind of chaotic movement that I felt was very close to my own feelings, to my own deepest wishes about fiction. It's one of the only films that I wish I could have made.

GM: So you've always been an experimenter in fact.
JC: It's necessary in order to stay alive.

GM: And you've tried different genres. What are you going to do now?
JC: I'm working on a novel in the form of an agenda, you know, with fifty-two chapters for fifty-two weeks and four seasons of the year. The novel will be illustrated by Jacques Loustal who is one of the best illustrators and authors of graphic novels in the world. I'm very, very pleased to be able to collaborate with him, and I'm working more and more with the relationship between words and images, and the kind of intertext or interface between both. Other people interface with computers; I'd rather interface with artists.

"Writing About":
An Interview with Jerome Charyn

Marc Chénetier / 1995

From *Dramaxes. De la fiction policière, fantastique et d'aventures*, ENS Editions, Fontenay/
St Cloud (1995): 113–28. Reprinted by permission of Marc Chénetier. Translated by Sophie
Vallas.

MC: What is the place of crime fiction in your work?

JC: I don't regard the books I write as belonging to a genre. There are so
many prejudices against that type of writing that it is difficult to move in and
out a genre. The only thing I can say is that as my brother happened to be a
police detective he was indeed able to give me elements thanks to which I
could create a sort of tapestry, a dynamics, thanks to the language and all the
paraphernalia that the police really use. I do not have the impression that
those books are in the least different from the other books I've written. The
only criterium is language itself, and the texture of language. If the language
collapses, the books collapse. From my point of view, I was trying to write
explosive texts whose heroes and heroines happened to be police people.
I think one of the difficulties most readers of traditional detective stories
come up against is the fact that they don't understand what the books are
all about.

In the first of those novels, *Blue Eyes*, the hero dies in the very middle of
the story and the novel goes on, which seems quite strange. Which means
that the true problem raised by the text is that the invention only starts
after the death of the hero. And what do you make of a text that only begins once the hero is dead? Not to mention the complete reinvention of the
hero through his death, as well as seven other novels whose invention rests
entirely on the pretext of this death. In my opinion this is exactly the same
kind of challenge that you find in *Pinocchio's Nose*. You may see in the novel
a rewriting of the legend of Pinocchio, whereas I see a form of parody of a

given literary genre. The word parody is crucial: one plays with a text and with a genre. And such a game is a success or a failure only depending on the power of language.

MC: In the 1950s you worked on the "voice project" with John Hawkes at Stanford. *The Lime Twig* dates back to that period. It is also a novel in which the character dies in the first chapters, a sort of criminal investigation. Do you see an influence on your own detective fiction?

JC: No, even if Hawkes did represent a powerful influence when I began to write. He was probably the best of all American writers because he pushed the language to extremes, and because he could perceive the silent cruelty of language. The point is not to compose a cruel story; the point is language itself and its potential of cruelty. *The Lime Twig* was an extraordinary text written by someone who had never set a foot in England and who could nevertheless grasp—and capture, so to say, in a parodic form—the precise language an Englishman could speak. His capacity to create a context thanks to imagination was amazing. Hawkes has never been an influence as far as narrative is concerned, but he has influenced me as far as language is concerned, undoubtedly.

For me there is no feeling in language. I believe that the potential of cruelty rests in a juxtaposition of words that is devoid of feeling, and that in Hawkes's very best texts there is no feeling. I remember a wonderful story he once told me: while he was in California after writing *Second Skin*, he went to visit his greatest fan, a prisoner in San Quentin. And this prisoner told him: "Listen, what you write is great, but I have the feeling that you're turning sentimental. Cut into the flesh or you're going to fall flat on your face," and this is exactly what happened since all of a sudden he gave this color to his language, he felt the necessity to obtain from language more than what it can give. If we go back to *The Lime Twig*, it's an amazing book because it is never judgmental, it only describes. I would draw a link between Hawkes and Dashiell Hammett. Crime fiction only starts with Hammett. Nobody could ever analyze what is at stake in his texts because when you look at his short stories, they're completely flat and stupid. Whereas when you take his first novel, *Red Harvest*, you can see an indescribable revolution. There is no visible stance taken on what is being described. There is an extraordinary sensitivity to the space between each sentence so that when you read the text, your imagination feeds not on the sentences but on the space between the sentences. This is where Hammett's considerable contribution is, and nobody has analyzed it yet. His short stories remain limited to the genre, they are rather shaky stories. But when you take the novels, and *Red Harvest* and *The Glass Key* especially, you suddenly find yourself in a very different world, a world which is in no way picturesque and which is not trying to mimic the gangsters of the 1920s. In his writing there is suddenly this extraordinary distance between sentences, between words themselves, and because adjectives are almost completely cut out, you get very naked, very dry and cruel sentences.

MC: You said you admire the fact that Hawkes uses language to build a whole world which is not familiar to him and that the result is even better than if he actually knew it. And yet you write using very familiar elements. I'm thinking of New York City.
JC: I admire those constructions of language, those cities of words, and it doesn't matter whether the author knows or not the place he describes. What is important is the idea of a pure, whole construction which manages to create or to re-create something. Walter Abish, in *Alphabetical Africa*, invents and reinvents a story only by going through the alphabet. In the first chapter there are only words starting with an A, in the second words starting by A or B, in the third words starting by A, B or C, and so on until he reaches the end of the alphabet. And then he takes away letters down to the initial A, and he does it while telling a story at the same time. To me—and even if people like Queneau did similar things—what this novel suggests is something in which I deeply believe, namely that language is completely artificial, and that one can say whatever one means even within the most rigid constraints. Abish, for that matter, manages to tell a stunning and frightening story in this most rigid framework. In a way this is what crime fiction is all about: very strict constraints which give birth to horror. That's what Hammett invented. It's not a matter of amnesia, but of a conscious reduction of language deliberately contained within certain limits, because such limits reinforce the impact and the emotional quality of what one means.

Denis Mellier: Is not this constraint that can be found in the framework of crime fiction the reason why crime fiction and contemporary fiction often meet—I'm thinking about Borges, Perec, Auster, or Ackroyd. The stricter the system of constraints, the more at stake the formal reinvention is, which could explain why many authors like to mix a more open form of literature with a form that is usually said to be closed upon itself?
JC: You're right. What you mean is that a sort of confusion occurs. I'd like to evoke a passage from a recent text by Joyce Carol Oates on detective fiction,

which raises the problem one generally stumbles on when talking about the genre. To sum up, she says that the essential characteristic of detective fiction is probably the creation of a pact between the author and the reader from the very first sentence on, and that a detective novel must not betray this initial commitment, that it must not crumble into ambiguity and irresolution, which is what the literary novel, in which real life collapses, does. And she goes on evoking some writers who drift away from this tradition, only to say that their examples are abnormal cases in what remains, she says, essentially a mass genre whose function is to quench an insatiable thirst for narratives whose plots entirely rest on action. She concludes by saying that the best traditional crime writers never allow themselves to get involved in form, because what's the point, she wonders. Inventiveness can give free rein to itself within the limits of the genre.

Such a statement could apply to 90 percent of crime fiction writers, who explore nothing, who exist within the genre by limiting the risks. But the same could be said about 90 percent of writers, whether they write crime fiction or not, who don't take risks, who make sure they have something to fall back on. So such a criterium cannot be used to define anything. The best writers, whatever the genre, are always those who play with the form, who work within limits and constraints, and who draw something new—except when they fail in their attempt. I think that modern writing chose two different directions, either an expansion of language, a proliferation of words—let's say Joyce, Faulkner, and Nabokov—or a contraction of language, a contraction that also allows you to create something new. In crime fiction, Hammett was the first one to show that language itself, when given very precise limits, could create something that has never been seen before.

DM: Have you kept in your writing formal constraints that are usually considered as inherent to crime fiction?

JC: I don't feel I'm facing constraints or restrictions. I don't see myself as operating within a framework. It so happens that my books deal with policemen and that there are therefore elements that are determined by their way of behaving. You can't turn them into heroes of the absurd and oblige them to catch criminals at the same time. The only constraint is linked to the methodology of criminal procedures—it's the only one I feel concerned by. *Secret Isaac*, for instance, is a sort of Joycean homage to my vision of Dublin, seen through the eyes of Joyce and through the prism of language. It becomes extremely difficult to pretend to describe any form of crime literature once you start considering it in terms of genre.

MC: But then if you don't acknowledge any of the constraints of the genre, how can you play with those limits and therefore with the possibility to go beyond them and to turn them into something else?

JC: I was speaking about the constraints of language. I intend to talk about only one thing, which is language. It's not by strengthening the picturesque or the vocabulary that you push language to extremes, it's only by setting limitations. That's the only difference. It's a way to abolish the bifurcation between the two directions I was mentioning previously: you can try to use language in order to obtain some effects, but it's through a loss in terms of vocabulary and not through an expansion of this vocabulary. It has nothing to do with the constraints of form. I don't think that this form exists in a purest state. If you take Paul Auster, or whoever else for that matter, the best texts are always a matter of language, period.

MC: How do you turn an infraction into something productive?

JC: If you're writing a crime novel, you can take it out of its context which is that of the elucidation of a crime. Okay! Then you fall into easy parody. Or else you think, no, a crime will indeed take place and will be solved, and I won't have much room for maneuver. But as I move in this narrow margin many things will take place, whether you can see and recognize them or not, and I'm not going to do it playfully, I'm going to do it threateningly. I'm going to build terror not on the crime itself and its resolution, but on all those side elements. The only interesting and important thing is to use the limits, whether they apply to your subject or to the context, to work them again and to turn them inside out in order to transform them into elements of power, of strength instead of elements of dispossession. I think that is what you always find in the best novels.

David McFarlane: In the preface to *Blue Eyes* you evoke very precise themes—this "gigantic combination of fathers and sons," for instance—but also a context and your desire to escape the genre. Everything is therefore not only a question of language.

JC: The label I mentally attach to it doesn't matter, and what the novel is linked to doesn't matter either. When I wrote *Blue Eyes*, my only obligation was to go from one sentence to the next, to create a sort of uninterrupted music that could carry you further into the text. I wrote this preface in order to try and explain why I was writing. I was at the time in the middle of a one-thousand-page novel that was completely devoid of music, and I was completely at a loss. How could I find the music back? I had the subject but no music to go along with it; I was powerless to find a language that could give it life, to find an interior landscape that could breathe life into this so-called subject I was writing about. I was able to do that in my crime novels because they were somehow parables of my own experience in relation to my brother. I was able to find the appropriate music to tell this story, and we could have an endless discussion about what this story is all about, but I will only say that a novel is working or not depending on its capacity to maintain the music or the language from the beginning to the end—what you could call the rhetoric.

The most interesting text in twentieth-century American literature is "The Pedersen Kid" by William Gass. If you look at the text closely I defy you to tell me what it is about, I defy you to sum it up. It's a text on nothingness, on the whiteness of nothingness! This text does not tell anything—it's all about the snow, empty spaces, the icing quality of language. Gass manages to tell you something, thanks to various sentences, about the joy you experience when discovering language, because it's one of his early texts and he will never find it again—it's something that happens only once. He can write the most perfect novel in the world, fifteen pages, two thousand pages. In fact it will happen to him a second time, in his essay about the color blue, because he explores and discovers the same thing again: I'm going to write about nothingness, about the blue of nothingness, and then you have the same kind of formal perfection, not only because you're dazzled—you can be dazzled by anything—but because it is so upsetting that he manages to carry you in that way to the limits of language.

And it's also a crime story, because in the end, when writing is at its best, there is always this lurking nihilism that suggests "what the heck?" After all, what's language? They say language is what enables us to communicate, but as far as I'm concerned, I think that very often it's exactly the other way round, language is what keeps us apart even more. It's the thing that keeps us at a distance, a necessary distance. I'm speaking about written language, not oral language, and we need that to survive. We would be unable to survive without such distance, it would be too frightening. Language is our second skin.

Language always finds its coherence around a subject. This is unavoidable. If it wasn't the case, we'd become crazy. We wouldn't be able to read language. One has to present a sort of formal image. The subject is inherent to language, otherwise it would be impossible to move forward. It's in the very nature of language to go from the abstract to the specific in order to create myths. In American mythology, it may be this confusion of fathers and sons. In English mythology it may be something else. But whatever the mythology may be, it is language only which, by operating around it, makes it work. A text operates in what I would call the substratum of the text, a sort of underlying emotional tonality that all text must possess and without which language would become uncertain or opaque.

Luc Ruiz: Why did you choose crime fiction to carry out this reflection on language and writing?

JC: Why do I write crime fiction? I would see a link with cinema here. It's a sort of democratic institution in which you don't have to bring your own stock of knowledge; you don't need any literary heritage to read crime fiction. You don't need a context, you don't need to know Joyce, you don't need any background to read those texts. It was a way for me to escape my own "literary heritage." It was like setting on another kind of journey for which I didn't have to present a mirror to the texts I had read before or to enter into a dialogue with other writers. It was for me the first somewhat "democratic" way of writing because you only needed your own intelligence, just as when you're watching a movie since movies undoubtedly create their own landscape, their own genre, their own vocabulary. This is why I believe that modern crime fiction only starts with the invention of cinema, of course, but also photography. I think photography is the perfect example of an image which has its own power and which, even when it has its own coloration, goes on existing in the most extreme and strict monochrome.

MC: Many contemporary writers use the detective or criminal framework in their texts [. . .] as a way to get rid of the "what it is about." The word "about," to me, can be seen as an indirect commentary on your own theory of composition. What I would call the "aboutness" of literature has nothing to do with the transitive use of the term. There is in English an intransitive use of "about," as in "one walks about" or "one dances about," two phrases which suggest a way of getting round, of dodging the issues, of being around instead of being inside. And it seems to me that your writing consists in "writing about," not "writing about anything," but "writing about."

JC: When John Hawkes speaks, I don't need to say what the text is speaking about. It's something you have to make explicit as the text becomes more and more difficult in our quest for meaning. I think that very often, as far as meaning is concerned, we find ourselves at the very heart of language, and that very often we make errors of judgment, and it's only thirty or forty years later that the key text suddenly emerges. This is what happened to Faulkner, or to Melville for that matter. A whole century went by before the values of a new century enabled us to grasp the terms of Melville's own language. The detective novel, the mystery is, in my opinion, specific to our century, and the enigma is not only a matter of language but a matter of all kinds of values, human possibilities, and human circumstances. And I think that the emergence of the genre was only possible thanks to the scientific revolution of the beginning of the twentieth century which enabled us to realize that the more we learn about something, the less we know about it. We are therefore in a lull of the twentieth century. We probably have to wait for new discoveries to take place in order for us to reexamine things that we thought we knew, but that we don't really know. And that is the major obstacle.

Cécile Bloc-Rodot: Would the quest of literature, and perhaps the quest of the crime novel, be to find precision "in the aboutness?"
JC: It's the closest you can get to a definition of the potential of language. But could we use this formula to describe an isolated text? If you take a novelist such as Bernard Malamud, you realize that in the awkwardness he shows when he manipulates language there is also a sort of power, a power that originates from this very awkwardness. The human quality often comes from an aspiration to precision and from the failure of such an aspiration.

David McFarlane: You insist on the democratic dimension of crime fiction while at the same time you keep referring to a literature that's very ambitious and complex, but that isn't popular.
JC: The texts that are not decipherable at a given moment very often end up opening up through indirect and perverse ways. Conversely, most of the texts that are successful when they are published very quickly fall into oblivion. The so-called best-sellers which have a tremendous impact at a given time no longer represent much twenty years later. The problem for best-sellers—and best-sellers can be great books, such as *One Hundred Years of Solitude*—is that language is literally absent from most of them. It's only content and not language. It's language at the service of content. It could be said that very often, any sentence read at a given time describes the world at that precise moment, even if you attempt to hide this, even if you're a twentieth-century writer who's trying to pass as an eighteenth-century writer. A writer always evokes his own time. That is why cinema offers the most convincing history of our century because even in a costume drama about Pompei or anything else, a moviemaker is describing the values, the drawbacks, and the virtues of his own time. That's where the power of cinema is. I think that

if you took a real film geek and that you had him listen to a soundtrack he would be able to give you the year the movie came out simply on the basis of the way people speak, because it's so revealing. The same holds true for language. Language is a sort of schizophrenic echo of what can happen at a given time. Only the twentieth century could invent crime fiction.

MC: Which brings us back to the importance of cinema in your conception of the novel and of writing.

JC: I grew up with cinema and the radio. The importance of music for me partly comes from the fact that I used to listen to the radio for hours, going from one type of show to another: historical dramas, adventure serials, and then Hollywood. And also from the fact that I was the product of a society or a culture which had absolutely no markers, which was powerless to understand the outside world. I belonged to a culture of immigrants that was unable to interpret the symbols of its own environment. It was a completely senseless situation. What language could you be willing to talk when there is no language? The only language I had was that of the radio, of the movies, period. At the time I wasn't interested in scriptwriters or moviemakers. To me the true authors of the movies were the actors—and I still believe in this. It's not only a matter of interpretation, it's the very presence of the actors which fashions and defines the texture of a movie. So that those heroes, once wrenched from the screen, reappear in my novels not as parodic figures but as real heroes.

Today we have this amazing luxury of being able to comfortably enter into a movie: you go to a movie theater, you know at what time the film is due to start, and you see it from the beginning. When I was a child, you never knew the times of the different showings, there was no program. You went in at seven and it was right in the middle of the movie. And I used to be able to say, word for word and without having seen it, what had happened in the beginning of the movie simply because by watching what followed, you ended up developing an intuitive sense of what came first. In other words a novel does not begin at the beginning of the novel. It starts somewhere around the middle, a middle that you create, and the beginning is somewhere but there is no need to write it down in black and white.

MC: Were you influenced by *film noir*?

JC: I'm not sure, but I think that its visual impact was considerable. I discovered cinema while *film noir* was at its highest. And what was especially striking was this juxtaposition of black, white, and grey that had never been seen on a screen before. All of a sudden it was a matter of finding the meaning not so much of the shadow but of the criss-cross of black, white, and grey lines. It was especially striking in a movie entitled *T-Men*: I'm probably one of the only persons in the world who saw it, but there was this crucial scene with a black and white blind that defined a sort of grey world. And the interpretation of this interpretation—not so much the fact that the world was seen through the blind, but the fact that the blind projected shadows onto something else—was enough to add a context that did not exist before: of course we had already seen things through a misted-up window pane, in a bright sunny day, in a rainy day, or in a misty day, but we had never seen reality thus criss-crossed by those bright black and white lines. And I think that this is what the *film noir* offered us: this extraordinary use of color without color. That is why I was unable to watch a Technicolor movie after having watched all those marvelous films in black and white. It seemed to be such a reduction of the material, such an *intrusion*.

So for me cinema was less a process of education than an incomparable means to hone my own tools. It was the perfect formation for a writer because today, much to my embarrassment, I can confess how many books I read before I turned eighteen: I started with *Pinocchio*, went on with *Bambi*, and then I read a few history books in school, but that was it. How did I dare to become a writer? When I finally went to the university and when I walked into the library for the first time, with this amazing labyrinth of books all around me . . . I'd love to be able to say today that it was Kafka, but no, it wasn't. It was Sophocles and Euripides. And I lost nothing by not having read them earlier. The kids I used to go to school with, who had read *War and Peace* at fourteen, never recovered from it! They were completely lost. To me, this is what American literature is all about: empty spaces that you appropriate in your own groping, mysterious way.

From New York to the *Polar*:
An Interview with Jerome Charyn

Goulven Hamel / 1995

From *Tempêtes sous un crâne* 7 (printemps-été 1995): 41–46. Reprinted by permission of Goulven Hamel. Translated by Sophie Vallas.

GH: In France you are essentially known as a New Yorker—a man who has been chronicling his hometown from the very beginning.

JC: The New York City I paint in my books is a sort of strange adventure, a mixture of imagination and daily life. This city is extraordinary because everything is possible there. It's the only city in the world in which you can walk around naked without anyone looking at you. In New York there is nothing like instinctive judgment, and to me, it is essential to be able to live according to one's own fantasy, no matter what forms it takes. I think it is very sane to exist without being constantly observed.

GH: In the *Isaac Quartet*, which was written in the 1970s, you denounce social problems such as injustice, misery, and corruption. Do you think the situation in New York has changed since that date?

JC: It is different today because in the 1980s, during Ronald Reagan's presidency, some people became a lot richer while poverty considerably increased. Remember, it's in New York that the first signs of such poverty became visible, with the sudden multiplication of homeless people. New York being the city of extremes, it was only logical for extreme situations to become even more extreme there. At the same time, and much to my surprise,

Polar is a French slang term for *roman noir* that both Goulven Hamel and Jerome Charyn keep using in this conversation and which is impossible to translate into English. It brings both a popular and subversive touch that Charyn often says he especially enjoys.

we have an excellent mayor today. I thought that Rudolph Giuliani would be very conservative and would be against the black population, for instance. But I was wrong. He has really developed a passion for this city and he has launched into necessary reforms and changes which are bringing about effects. This city is fascinating because it demands a feeling for perspective, a vision of its future and of its own universe, and once again, I think that it is proper to New York. Elsewhere, politicians can deliver speeches and make promises. But in New York, you can actually take action. Even if you cannot solve all the city's problems, you can nevertheless really tackle them and find ways of doing so, and to me, this is very important.

GH: In your books you often mention the role and the importance of the Mafia in New York, and one can have the feeling that you are sometimes fascinated by the figure of the gangster.

JC: Fascination is not the exact word. You must keep in mind that, until very recently, the Mafia paradoxically played a very important role as far as maintaining order in the city was concerned. I don't want to criticize the police, but very little was done as far as the prevention of daily crimes and murders was concerned. Conversely, in neighborhoods controlled by the Mafia, there were no murders. Unfortunately the federal government infiltrated the Mafia and arrested a lot of street captains, and this only added to chaos without solving anything. New York is a city of chaos. You need a tremendous energy to fight against chaos and I think that in its own ways, the Mafia possesses such energy. Of course they are criminals, they kill each other and steal from everyone. But on the other hand, if you leave them alone, they leave you alone.

GH: You've been living part-time in Paris for years now. You said recently that you wouldn't be able to write about another city than New York with the same intimacy. Do you think that one day you'll write a novel that takes place in Paris?

JC: Even if I've been observing things about Paris, whatever I could say about it will never be as interesting as what someone who was born and grew up there could write, someone who has the city's colors, smells, and atmosphere in their minds. I think it would feel very artificial for me to try and do the same. Perhaps I could write a play, because it would be more abstract, or a graphic novel. Yes, I will probably write a scenario on Paris for a graphic novel, but I won't write a novel.

GH: You keep coming back to some of your characters, such as Sydney Holden or Isaac Sidel in spite of the fact that you don't seem to have the idea of a whole cycle in mind when you create them. Would you agree with the idea that you sometimes write "open novels" and sometimes "closed novels?"

JC: Yes I do. I firmly believe in a sort of alternative between paradox and schizophrenia. One constantly find oneself right in the middle of those opposite forces—what you call "open forms" and "closed forms," which are, in fact, very similar to each other. When I start writing a new book, it contains its own internal mystery. Even if I take up a character I used before, the enigma, the internal puzzle of the book will be different. Take *Paradise Man* or *Elsinore*, for instance: the characters are the same, and yet to me the novels are extremely different. To me, the essential thing is this puzzle which characterizes each book. You have to create a tension, both in the language and in the plot, and then you have to deal with it.

GH: Your characters look alike, they seem to have the same vital energy, they come from a similar background and they share a lot of features. Could you give a definition of a Charynian character?

JC: I think characters come to life when they find their names. To me, the name defines a character. Usually what happens is that the character finds a kind of rhythm from that moment on, a physical appearance and then a voice, with a music of its own. Now, if you consider the characters as ghosts that get born in a same mind, a little like phantoms coming from the same "closed world," then their fabrication process is no longer that strange. Some writers use five, six, seven characters maybe in order to create a story. I tend to use two hundred characters. In one of my books which hasn't been published in France yet, *War Cries over Avenue C*, there are five, six, seven characters on each page! The characters finally compose something like psychological colors, the colors on a same palette, and the process is the same as when you enter into a painting or a music piece. What is essential for me is the image, what you see and what you hear. If you think about a character in such a way, then he is bound to be very different from the character in a traditional novel, a creature which is determined by a psychological profile—is he married, does he have children?— and which finds its definition in such a profile. My characters are never determined in such a way; they are always defined by a sort of suffering. They are determined by a pain, an internal suffering, and it's radically different.

GH: To borrow your own words, Isaac Sidel has been "screaming in your head" for seven novels. What kind of relationships have you developed with such a character that has been haunting you for twenty years?

JC: The first book I wrote in which Isaac Sidel appeared was *Blue Eyes* even if, chronologically, *Marilyn the Wild* comes before in the saga, although it was written after. Isaac was only a minor character in *Blue Eyes*, and he remains in the margins in the second and third volumes (*The Education of Patrick Silver*). It was only in the fourth volume, *Secret Isaac*, that Isaac emerges and that the novel became his. What happens today (and to go back to what I was saying a few minutes ago), is that Isaac now owns a music which is closest to mine, which is most intimate to me. I discovered Isaac thirty years ago. Now he's my age, he has the same weaknesses as I have and perhaps also the same strength. I am no longer the same person, I no longer have the same interests in life, and I feel very close to him. That's why I go on writing about Isaac.

GH: Speaking about *Secret Isaac*, it is easy to see that this novel is different from the others in the saga: it's stranger, much more complex, and it has a different music. Can it be described as a sort of turning point in the cycle? Why is it so different from the preceding and following novels?

JC: When I started to write novels, I was a very "experimental" writer, to use a word which should be used by critics. I developed forms that were very abstract, both in my mind and on the page. The novels that were written before the *Isaac Quartet* are what you could call postmodern fiction. In a way, having written those novels represented a form of training which allowed me to write in a more personal and, paradoxically perhaps, in a more *abstract* way. And I do think that I need to have those two forces interact in my writing. For instance, if the book is too personal, it lacks this efficiency, this power in its construction and it becomes simply sentimental. If I hadn't gone through those six or seven writing exercises, I don't think that, in *Blue Eyes*, I would have been able to cope with this mixture of elements which are both terrifying and very close to me. Abstraction and intimacy—both are indispensable. In a way, I finally found the kind of universe which possessed the intensity that I needed, which possessed its own personal might, its own energy and weaknesses.

GH: Your main characters are essentially men. And yet there are a lot of women in the shadows, whose presence is very important for the novels. But the foreground is occupied by men.

JC: That's true. But *Darlin' Bill* is about a woman, and in other novels, such as *The Tar Baby* for instance, there are very important and central female characters. But this could be something I have to explore more—to enter deeper into female characters, to understand their psychology. I may be reaching a limit here. I don't know, it's difficult to say. At the moment, for instance, I'm writing a memoir about my mother. Perhaps this will change things for me and allow me to go further into female characters.

GH: *Panna Maria* is a truly fascinating novel.
JC: Yes, I think it's my best. You have to read it in English though, for I'm not very happy with the French translation.

GH: Precisely, what are your relationships with your translators? In France, you've been working a lot with Cécile Bloc-Rodot, who has recently translated some of your work as well as your chronicles in the weekly magazine published by *Libération.*
JC: Yes, my work has been translated by Cécile and also by Marc Chénetier, in France. I also have an excellent translator in Germany and in Italy. It has become a very important thing for me, an essential thing even. It's very difficult to translate my books because I have a very strange language. It doesn't fit into any literary tradition. It uses elements that come from elsewhere. It is therefore very difficult for a translator to find equivalents in their own language. It demands a lot of plasticity from them. But to go back to *Panna Maria*, the book reverberates in many very different directions. It tells part of my own story, my background, the New York I come from. In a way, while I was writing *Panna Maria*, I discovered my own father, my grandfather, their stories. I reinvented them, I rediscovered them, I awakened them deep inside of me. And I really think that all those things that come from one's personal background, one's past, are much more important than the present or the future.

GH: At what precise moment do you know that you have the beginning of a plot on the page? In your preface to *Blue Eyes*, you evoke the moment in the story when the book escaped you to go and follow its own road. But when you're working, at what moment can you say, "Ok, this is the beginning of something?"
JC: You have an idea in mind, and what you have to do is find the language that fits it as perfectly as possible—that is what comes first to me. Writing a novel thus resembles a strange journey in my eyes, a journey you experience

with your eyes closed, being blind to the world that surrounds your mind, because if you knew where the end of the journey will leave you . . . Let's take *Panna Maria*, for instance. I had absolutely no idea where the novel was going. Some readers say: "I can't follow you in such a strange journey." But others, on the contrary, will say: "OK, I allow you to take my hand and I'm going with you, because I want to believe in the path you're taking." Those are the readers I need, people with a certain faith, people who believe in the path I've chosen and who are willing to follow it with me. It's really strange, a little like a journey towards death: nobody really knows what is beyond death either.

GH: As *Panna Maria* once again testifies, you often make use of the material of your origins—the Bronx ghetto, the traditions of the Jewish community, Poland, the status of the minorities in New York—all those elements that have directly or indirectly participated in the construction of who you are now. But what are your links with the Jewish community today?
JC: Obviously I grew up in that community. My parents were both observant Jews who went to the synagogue. But what I found fascinating about being a Jew in New York did not imply something "religious," at least not in the usual meaning of the word. It meant a certain moral sense, a certain sense of justice, it meant being aware of poverty, believing in education, education for everyone, as well as in the necessity to fight against prejudice. I think that is fundamental, that we all have to fight against an evil which we all have deep within ourselves and which whispers in our ears that we are better than others—it isn't true. Perhaps as good as others. I think the most important thing that the Jews have brought to New York (not only the Jews, but the Jews more than anybody else) is this sense of fairness, especially as far as education is concerned. Fifty or sixty years ago, New York used to have some of the best schools in the world, and I'm speaking about public schools, not private ones. Today we have some of the worst because the situation has completely changed. I was lucky enough to grow up in a period when everything was still possible. I said that I wanted to become a writer, and such a statement had nothing to do with money or the desire to have a career, to have a social status. It was just what I wanted to do, and I think that at the time I was allowed to say: "Yes, you can do it," and it has nothing to do with money or anything else like that. I doubt such a thing is still possible today. I'm not saying it's impossible, I'm just saying that I'm not sure that if I grew up in New York today, I could afford the luxury to say the same thing. It was what I really wanted to do, and I was allowed to do everything I

could to reach my aim. Even to make mistakes, because if you're not allowed to make mistakes, you cannot succeed, you cannot experiment.

GH: You spend part of the year in Paris now. Your readers have always felt how important Europe was in your work, which is not that usual for American writers.

JC: I have the feeling that I'm accomplishing the return travel of my parents, who once left Russia and Poland. And I don't mean Russia in itself or Poland in itself, in fact I mean Europe, a word which sounds in a very special way to my ears. People do not really understand how close to the culture of New York City European culture is. New York is truly a European city, it is absolutely not an American city. You have to keep that in mind. It's not a Catholic city, it's not a Protestant city, it's a city that literally came out of Europe. Today, the situation may be a little different, but when I grew up, it was a deeply European city. So when I came to Europe, it was the first time that I felt at home in a place other than New York. The first place I settled in was Madrid, then Barcelona, then Paris. It's not just Paris, therefore, but several countries, Mediterranean countries.

GH: You are a marginal. You're Jewish but you had problems with orthodox Jews because of some of your satirical novels; you're American but you say you're in fact a New Yorker, a New Yorker who has found his roots in Europe; you write *polars* but they tend to explode their own frames, they belong only to you and to your own language; you are a fan of comic books and graphic novels. In the end, you look like Isaac himself, who, as you once wrote, keeps dancing on the extreme edge of legality.

JC: Or maybe I look like a catfish. Writing is just like living, a mere trace footprint left on the sand. Just lay your hand on the sand, and you won't be able to see anything at first. It will take a long time to discover where the print is, and who knows, another person might see it red. I have no idea. It seems to me that there is a particular pattern, a very specific vision, perhaps an unconscious one, but which is nevertheless present in every work. People might discover it, and again they might not. Perhaps the print left on the sand will have disappeared or, on the contrary, perhaps it will have become even more visible. It's very difficult for me to phrase it, and it's not for me to do it anyway. I can't be the interpreter of what I write. I write all this because that's what I like to do, what I want to do and that's it. For instance there are a very few writers, a very few American writers who write graphic novels. They don't understand anything about it. In my eyes, and of course this is a very personal opinion, France is *the* place for graphic novels in the world, what you call *bande dessinée*. It is where the greatest artists can be found, and if they're not French themselves, they're never far away from here. Can you image artists such as Muñoz, Loustal, or Boucq, the very best in the world, in the U.S.? It has been an incredible pleasure for me to work with them. Now some people tell me: "But why on earth have you written those graphic novels? Why don't you keep to novels?" My aim was precisely to try and make the intensity of a novel fit into a graphic novel. I stick to what I want to do, the rest is unimportant. I may be right, I may be wrong, but I think I'm right.

GH: You've just mentioned American writers in general. But you have been writing *romans noirs* for quite a long time, and you must have noticed that the most inventive, interesting, brilliant writers, those who may come closer to a certain truth of what the modern novel is today, have all a link with *polar*. Would you agree?

JC: I agree. But once again, I don't think people really understand what *polar* is. And I think that the French are those who come closest to understanding it. The reason why it has not been understood is that it introduces quite a particular language, and there isn't anything more difficult to discuss than language. Nobody has managed to do it, in my opinion. I wrote a text for Gallimard, for an anthology entitled *Le Nouveau Noir*, a text in which I try to define what such a language expresses. Daniel Pennac is part of the anthology. Criticism is a strange thing, for one single person is in charge of illuminating a text. And if such a person fails to do so, if the text has not been celebrated the way it should be, then it is going to drift away where nobody will see it anymore. The genre of *polar* has never had the critical fame it deserves. Perhaps one day it will get it, I don't know.

GH: What are you reading at the moment? Who are the French authors you feel closest to? You've just mentioned Daniel Pennac, and recently Didier Daeninckx.

JC: Pennac is the one I know the most. And Benacquista too. I read more and more in French. But if you go backwards, I've always loved Rimbaud and I do think he's one of the greatest, the way he battles with language. I've always found there was a very destructive element in French, the word *"de"* ... You keep having to use it. English is a much more elastic language. French has a structure which is almost unbreakable, even if people, like Céline for example, have perfectly managed to break it. It's one of the main difficulties people meet when translating my books. When the translation is over, I see this whole, parallel structure, and I don't want to see it because it looks meaningless to me. I want the translator to destroy this structure, to pull it down. As I'm reading more and more in French, I might be able to tell you more in a few years. But for the moment, the French authors I read most are Daniel Pennac, Didier Daeninckx, and Tonino Benacquista, and I also greatly admire Céline and Genet.

An Interview with Jerome Charyn

David Seed / 1995

From *Over Here* 15.1–2 (summer-winter 1995): 113–14. Reprinted by permission of David Seed.

DS: Most of your fiction is set in New York. Could you say a little about what sort of place it is and what possibilities it opened up for your novels?

JC: New York has always been the city where *anything* can happen, where night, day, sun, moon, wind, and rain are all part of one crazy, looping atmosphere. I tried to catch their rhythm in my own writing, this curious snake dance of the city where Melville's Bartleby was born. New York is the home of the hangman and the artist, and I'm not sure which is the deadlier of the two.

DS: Certainly your New Yorkers are always unpredictable and I could never see the logic of calling your early works "local color." How easy did you find it to publish your fiction? Did you feel that the literary scene in the early sixties was at all excluding the kind of novels you wanted to write?

JC: I had nothing to do with the literary scene. I didn't know *any* other writer. I sent off a story to *Commentary* ("Faigele the Idiotke"), and the magazine decided to publish it—which seemed like an utter piece of magic.

DS: In fact I thought I spotted some resemblances between *Once upon a Droshky* and some of Isaac Babel's stories, maybe an analogy between Babel's Odessa and your New York. Was Babel or Isaac Singer, for instance, an influence on your works?

JC: I adore Isaac Babel. When I first read the Odessa stories and *Red Cavalry*, I found my mentor; the stories were warm and *killing* at the same time. I discovered Babel while I was writing *Once upon a Droshky*, and I'm sure there is a resemblance. I'd also read one of Singer's stories, "Gimpel the

Fool." But Singer didn't have Babel's precision, Babel's *modernity*—his insistence that language is an instrument of pain.

DS: That sounds as if it could be disconcerting for the reader. The critic Albert J. Guerard has found what he calls a "distrust of established novel form" in your works. Does that match your own sense of your writing?

JC: I distrust all established forms. The novel has a kind of plasticity that's almost *outside* form; its music can and should take the reader anywhere.

DS: And your characters too can end up anywhere. I have been struck again and again with your sympathetic portrayal of outlaws, racketeers, and characters who seem to be outside the political power structure. Was this conscious on your part and at all connected with your interest in child's-eye perspectives? I believe you were working for a time on a book called *A Child's History of the Bronx.*

JC: I love outlaws. I feel like an outlaw. I think the writer has to push as hard as he (or she) can against the established culture. The outlaw always has this childish belief in the possibility of *self*. The racketeer is something else. He preys upon the culture, creates his own form of chaos. Language itself is outside the law—it's dangerous, full of contradictions: practical and impractical at the same time.

DS: You have said that in *Eisenhower, My Eisenhower* you found your voice. What did that involve? Would you describe that novel as science fiction fantasy in any sense?

JC: *Eisenhower* is the most autobiographical book I've ever written, even though it's about gypsies who fuck with their tails. It has all the chaotic rhythms that were babbling inside my head: it attacks, withdraws, attacks again. It's like that marvelous comic book character, Plastic Man, who can bend around corners, contend with any surface by simply reshaping himself.

DS: And your novels too seem to be "plastic," in the sense of reshaping themselves constantly. How important was your discovery of writers like Hawkes and Nabokov for your own career?

JC: Hawkes was incredibly important to me; he was the first writer I'd read who was playing with anti-novels, texts that refused to go anywhere, that had their own slippery structure. I also loved Nabokov and love him now. His music is absolute, but his language is a little too literary. He wasn't living on the other side of the moon, with John Hawkes.

DS: I believe you met Hawkes while taking part in the Voice Project. What was that exactly?

JC: The Voice Project was an attempt to create young writers through an exploration of the spoken voice—that is, each writer had an essential music that was *discoverable*. It was a wonderful, crazy, idyllic idea. I taught in the Voice Project for two semesters while I was at Stanford.

DS: In the early seventies you were coediting *Fiction* with Donald Barthelme. Were you looking for any particular sort of fiction there?

JC: We were looking for any kind of writing that could excite us. It was Barthelme's own aura that was able to draw many writers to us: Barth, Handke, etc. I was even able to get a piece out of John Lennon.

DS: There's a very funny parody of academic journals in *The Tar Baby*. Did anything specific trigger that parody? I was also wondering how your relations with the academic community have developed over the years.

JC: I'd read a special issue on T. S. Eliot in the *Sewanee Review*, if I remember right, and I felt that there was a novel hidden within the crazy form of festschrift. I wasn't only thinking of academic communities, but of *any* community, which has its own warlike structure.

DS: You've recorded your interest in film in *Movieland*. Have you drawn on movies at all in shaping your novels or been involved in any filming projects?

JC: I have been a co-producer and co-writer for a telefilm based on *The Good Policeman*. And I might even find a way to copy that in my own fiction, but I've been a moviegoer since the age of five. I'm sure it has influenced my novels, even shaped them, but it's a bit too reductive for me to talk about this.

DS: Have you found any contemporary writers who you feel are working in areas similar to your own? I noticed, for instance, a Stanley Elkin title (*George Mills*) is woven into *Pinocchio's Nose* and you have recently recorded your appreciation of Elkin's self-mocking humor.

JC: The book I feel closest to is Leonard Cohen's *Beautiful Losers*—a wild, wooly journey into the bloodiest heart of our times. There's no logic to the text, only structured feelings. I mentioned George Mills in *Pinocchio's Nose* because the opening of Stanley's book is a wonderful, inventive trip through some medieval land, and I was trying to imagine Mussolini's own *medievalism* in much the same way.

DS: There seemed to be a big change in your works when you moved from fantasy into detective novels in the 1970s. What was it that made you decide to shift over into crime fiction?

JC: My brother was a homicide detective, a sad killer angel, and I wanted to write about this killer angel, so I invented Manfred Coen in *Blue Eyes*. But the killer angel himself is killed, and so I had to continue Coen's story, invent a history for him, which included his bearlike, brutal chief, Isaac Sidel.

DS: That Isaac Sidel series has now been going for a good twenty years. *Maria's Girls* was the last one to come out in Britain. How much further do you think the series will go?

JC: The series will change as the times and Isaac Sidel change—and as long as the characters continue to move me. I was much younger than Isaac when the series began; now I'm older, and he's become my own crazy comrade.

DS: You've had a base in Paris for a number of years. Are you conscious of any differences between the ways the French respond to your writings and the Americans?

JC: The French are the only readers in the world who are real "amateurs" of crime fiction; they understand its metaphysics and its limits—and they were able to see how I'd twisted the whole genre around and stood it right on its head.

DS: Fairly recently you started producing graphic novels. Could you say what aroused your interest in the form and also where your plans lie for future works?

JC: For me graphic novels are a logical extension of words themselves, of the images locked up in words. I love to read them and to write them. The best of them are completely removed from the deadening reality of most novels and films. I'm currently working with José Munoz, who is among the very best graphic novelists on the planet. He sculpts images in black and white with a marvelous, chilling abstraction. The story is about a female homicide detective in the Bronx who's also a bodybuilding queen. She's searching for her brother, a high school principal, who's become the personal slave of a druglord in Chile . . .

Jerome Charyn

Frederic Tuten / 2004

From *BOMB Magazine*, Issue 89 (Fall 2004): 56–61. © BOMB Magazine, New Art Publications and its Contributors. All rights reserved. The BOMB Digital Archive can be viewed at www .bombsite.com. Reprinted by permission of Charles Day.

FT: For how long and why are you living in Paris now?

JC: I bounce between Paris and New York like a crazed Ping-Pong ball. I think that for all precociously retarded kids from the Bronx (you might agree), growing up on movies and comic books, Paris was the one magic quotient that we would ever have: How could I forget Charles Boyer in *Arch of Triumph*? Or Bogart hiding out in Rick's Café, lisping about his lost love, Ingrid Bergman, and their little moments of romance in a Paris that was fragile and perfect, with the Germans about to vandalize it and Ingrid? The Bronx had the Loew's Paradise and a zoo, but Paris had Bogart's dreamy face and that gigantic metal ladder, the Eiffel Tower. I began living there part of each year in 1988, I fell in love with a beautiful one-eyed lady, and when that didn't work out I began teaching film at the American University in the seventh arrondissement, where I could see the Eiffel Tower twist and turn along the rue Saint-Dominique. I'm crazy about my students, who are orphans like me, running from their very own version of the Bronx. But when I'm not teaching or playing in Ping-Pong tournaments, I run right back to New York.

FT: Has living abroad changed or influenced your writing? After all, so many of your books have been set in New York City and particularly the Bronx—or "El Bronx" as you call one of your novels—that one would think you would need to keep living in New York for your sense of place.

JC: Living abroad has changed my writing. I feel like an amnesiac in relation to my own language. I forget five or ten words every day. I'm losing vocabulary like a man who's growing bald. It's terrifying. But it also gives me a curi-

110

ous strength. You have to go deeper into your memory to find the words that you need. And the Bronx has remained that country of childhood where you can invent your own vocabulary. I visit the old neighborhood as often as I can, sometimes with friends who love that little Italian enclave on Arthur Avenue, with its indoor market and restaurants where everyone eats at one communal table and the waiter brings you a bill without ever tallying what you ate. "El Bronx" is there inside my head, and I revisit it the way Hemingway would fish the Big Two-Hearted River in his dreams. I've captured the Bronx, I own it, and it remains in my imagination, like a prehistoric thing that's much deeper than culture or romance.

FT: *The Green Lantern*, your most recent novel, is set during one of the worst and most repressive periods in Soviet history. What made you, so long after the fact, want to write such a novel?

JC: I'm half Russian, and when I first read Dostoyevsky or Gogol, it was like falling upon a beloved crazy brother. (I felt that way with Faulkner, so he must have some Russian blood.) But when I first encountered Stalin in some newsreel during World War II, with his mustache and his one withered arm, I could have been looking at my father or some other madman out of my childhood. He was like a character in a fairy tale—cruel, inarticulate, whose only language was his fists. Stalin was the man who mumbled, and I loved the idea of a dictator without a vocabulary. I considered him as my very own little father. And when a friend of mine told me the story of how Stalin would sneak an actor into the Kremlin in the middle of the night and have him sing out the whole of *King Lear*, while he himself wept, I thought, Ah, that's the beginning of a novel!

FT: Although I know you've done it in several of your books, could you speak a little bit about your childhood in the Bronx? I should say *our* childhood in the Bronx—after all, wasn't that our playground?

JC: You ask me if the Bronx was my playground, when both of us know that it was a little paradise of empty spaces, a garden where nothing would grow, except bitterness and regret. I had one book in the house. The first volume of an encyclopedia that must have been sent to my parents as some sales trick—it was a treatise on the letter "A." And so I memorized that book, starting with aardvark, and could sing out to you all the manifestations of "A." Then my language stopped. And years later, when I read Walter Abish's *Alphabetical Africa*, I wondered if he too had started life with the same encyclopedia, but had been privileged enough to have more than one volume, since he could go all the way to "Z." And here I am, like some wily pirate, trapped inside the letter "A." Well, that's the Bronx. I wonder why my apartments in Paris and New York resemble Raskolnikov's closet. Both apartments are in luxurious buildings in classic neighborhoods—Montparnasse and Greenwich Village—but they're absolutely sparse, without much furniture at all. Does this void recall the void of growing up in the Bronx, where there was little "furniture" in the street—that is, nothing that could ever catch the eye? Is this "desert" more comfortable for me, and did it force me a long, long time ago to live inside my head? I must have been a novelist at five and six, or perhaps I was a walking, talking text, sucking in the movies I saw, the stories I heard, and the adventures of my older brother, Harvey, one of the boldest boys in the East Bronx, a Casanova at nine, prepared to take on any gang, a knight guarding his own turf, while I was frightened of anything beyond the reach of my nose, and lived only to imagine, to invent out of the nothingness I knew. Harvey would become a homicide detective, a catcher of cases, and I was the one who killed people off, the prince of an altogether different realm, a tumbler of words, who could only be adventurous on the page.

FT: What do you think, Jerry, has sustained our friendship all these years, considering neither of us is the adventurous sort?

JC: We've known each other fifty years, at least, starting out as rivals for the affection of Fay Levine, the Bronx's own Delilah, who was already a woman at twelve and had more admirers than one could possibly count; she couldn't ride a train or get on a bus without making a couple of conquests. But isn't it strange that you and I, coming out of a similar void, should be devoted to the diabolism of language, to all its nasty tricks, like some Natty Bumppo delving deeper and deeper into the forest? Where did we get such stamina in a world that is mostly indifferent to the written word? My original heroes weren't Faulkner and James Joyce. They were the Crapanzano brothers, in their flared, flamingo-colored pants, hoodlums with a sense of style. And perhaps Faulkner inherited the Crapanzanos' flair, in my own mind, an outlaw with absolute pitch, and his own flamingo-colored pants.

FT: All the same, we were both raised in a culture that loved books. That culture seems so far away today.

JC: We seem to live in a culture that has moved away from the idea of the "book" as a cherished item, or artifact, an imprint of our time. It's not so easy to explain why this happened. I think the culture is geared toward instant success, instant recognition; books have to bear the burden of becoming a bonanza, part of a hit parade. We've forgotten that each book is an eccentric affair; if we kill the notion of the eccentric, we will spawn books that have no voice, that are like faint little ghosts already invisible as they arrive. It's hard to judge what new art forms will inhabit our new century: I still believe in the power of fiction to tease us, hold us in its thrall; I still believe in the dancing rhythms of a text, in the curious river that runs from page to page; the romance of discovering Nabokov, reading Grace Paley's little urban time bombs, William Gass's frozen tar baby, called the Pedersen Kid, your own strange adventures of Chairman Mao on a long march that never seems to end, Don DeLillo's Harvey Oswald, who's one more orphan from the Bronx on a subway ride to nowhere, Donald Barthelme's Dead Father, who's bound to every child with a fierce cable, or Hemingway's Mrs. Macomber, a dia-bolic Annie Oakley, ready to kill a husband who needs killing. These books and authors have given me incredible delight. And I hope to hell that new masters will come along and feed me with some of the same.

FT: Maybe your new nourishment will come from movies, which you so love.

JC: The filmmaker I feel closest to is the Tarantino who made *Pulp Fiction*, who changed the whole format of cinema by reversing the order of sight and sound, forcing us to see with our ears and hear with our eyes. *Pulp Fiction* is a comic masterpiece where dialogue has a visual pull and the camera shies away from fancy footwork; it's there to hold the characters within the frame, to protect them as they present their own little riffs. Tarantino offers us a kind of parody that's never been shown on film—he attacks and defends at the same time, kisses and kills, so that when Christopher Walken as the ex-POW talks to us about the watch he had to hold up his ass, we laugh at the absurdity but never doubt his own weird logic. There are no safety zones in Tarantino; nothing is irrevocably written on the screen: John Travolta is blown away and then comes back and forth in his own liquid time frame. Tarantino says he doesn't believe in flashbacks, he's pivoting in time the way a novelist would pivot. In fact, *Pulp Fiction* is much closer to the novel's freedom than to the screen's frozen contemporaneity.

FT: Speaking of the novel again. The novel was born free, but everywhere I see it in chains. The novel's amplitude and invention, its open-endedness now seem molded into rigid and predictable forms. I know wonderful young writers who have no idea of the novel's generous heritage and have had no idea of how far afield, outside the predictable boundaries, they could fly.

JC: Why is it that neither of us ever got involved in realistic fiction? Your novel, *The Adventures of Mao on the Long March*, overwhelmed me because it was a battle cry against the quotidian and the commonplace—a novel that insisted on its own unique architecture, with the understanding that architecture is all. Yet where did this come from? I had no training in theory, nor did I ever write love letters to "form." I read Faulkner and saw that there was something more powerful than narrative itself—a driving belief in language and the notion that rhetoric was like a long snake put there to overcome the reader, seduce him or her into a kind of wondrous sleep, so that we could dream our way through *The Sound and the Fury*.

FT: It's not as if you've devoted yourself to a floating, free form of language at the expense of narrative. I think what you are talking about is a kind of magic within a structure.

JC: Perhaps the feeling for form came from reading comic books, which are all about architecture as we moved from panel to panel in a world that defied the "everyday," and was surreal without ever being conscious of it. I learned how to read from reading comic books, but you had to read in a very original way, absorbing the fury of each panel while you went on to the next. I'm not sure I would ever have wanted to write novels if I hadn't started comics. In fact, I see the novel as a kind of three-dimensional comic book, where the locale can change abruptly and where the characters can transform themselves from page to page.

FT: Well, movies were also comic books for us. Comic books in the dark.

JC: Both of us lived like lunatics at the Loew's Paradise. The Paradise was perfect for kids without a real center of gravity. We could fill up the empty spaces of the Bronx with Lana Turner and John Garfield, and with all the devilishness of film noir, which seemed much closer to me than the clotted cream of musical comedies. We became "readers" of film at an early age, not because we understood romance, but because we could intuit that Lana's movements, and the dimensions of her face, had more to do with a kind of hypnotic visual music than with narrative. So it now seems to me that we were much more sophisticated, much more alert, than all those kids of the middle class who crowed about Salinger's next story in the *New Yorker*, or about the MoMA and Matisse—we were more Matisse than they would ever be. Our museums were on the movie-house wall.

FT: Count me out here. The museum was my museum, especially MoMA, in its quiet days when I could see paintings and sit in the sculpture garden and read all day. Then the Bronx was far away. We've both tried to invent our own worlds, but we have taken our constructs from different sources.

JC: I think about the craziness of language and all its quests—not only to recapture and to reinvent, but to become a world unto itself. I'm writing a novel about Benedict Arnold, but how to enter the landscape, how to find a vocabulary and a music that will return to America and Manhattan in 1777? I read "contemporary" texts, such as the diary of Admiral Lord Richard Howe's secretary, Ambrose Serle, pick at words that delight me, such as *poltroon* and *molestation*, or the picture of George Washington as a "little paltry colonel of militia at the head of a banditti of rebels." And then I crawl into the whirlwind, into the music and the phrases. And my revolutionary America is a reflection of a world that might have been, but is also a strange new object, a toy of words, a monster of my own Little America, and perhaps that is what all texts are—monstrosities that overpower the real, that take over like creatures from some perverse private planet, that are much more infinite than the words they describe.

FT: Apropos again of language, hasn't living in France as long as you have affected your English, your sense of its contemporary usage (and misusage), affected your living in its familiar ocean?

JC: Yes, living in France has elongated my English, stretched it into a kind of perverse rubber band. I have to survive on my own inner ear, invent a meta-language that is mostly English, but also has a lot of Rimbaud and Baudelaire, and the little compositions in kindergarten French that I have to prepare for my landlord and my concierge if I want to make myself understood at all. I've remained a child within a French culture that demands precision and a sense of style, when all I can do is bumble around and hide my absence of grammar. So I feel like a commando in Paris, a night warrior, who guards whatever English he can while he loses words day by day in a battle against amnesia. But one thing is pronounced: I've retained and strengthened the vocabulary I had as a child when I roamed the Bronx like a little werewolf. And I've always felt that you are completely formed as a linguist by the time you're five. The mold is there, and you fill it with bits and pieces of vocabulary. And so in some strange way, isolation and exile have strengthened me as a writer, even though they've weakened my hold on words. I think your dreams are much more ferocious the further you fly from home.

FT: The two of us were born and raised in the Bronx, not too far from each other. We both carry El Bronx in us. I never write about it, running from its sadness and its stink by writing about characters and places far away—Van Gogh, Tallien, Tintin; China, France, South America. With several exceptions such as *The Green Lantern*, you write about the Bronx all the time. Which one of us is more haunted?

JC: You devil, didn't you call yourself the Bronx Racine, the Poussin of feelings, when you wrote about your father Rex in *Tallien: A Brief Romance* (of the Bronx)? I'm only teasing. We're both haunted in much the same way—running from the Bronx's sadness and its stink and its terrifying void. But I can feel that void in all your books. You write about China with the architecture of the Bronx and its endless dunes. And I run from the Bronx by trying to bring a lyrical touch to its madness, its black hole. I wrote about cavaliers—crooked policeman in orange pants, like Babel's Benya Krik, detectives who die while playing Ping-Pong, warlords who have no other language than their own battle cry. It's as if time froze around me (and you, I think), and the songs we sing to soothe ourselves have a very slanted rhythm. But it is strange. I travel up to the Bronx at least twice a year, and I feel powerful on its streets, like a figure out of Chagall who can float above the landscape, feel sexy, and take revenge on all those who thought they were so privileged because they grew up in the maw of Manhattan, went to museums, memorized *War and Peace*, while I was dreaming Tolstoy at five or six, without ever having read him.

FT: What made you decide to write this current novel about Russia in the Stalin period, when, after all, in the minds of many, that time and its issues are dead history?

JC: Stalin isn't dead history; he haunted my childhood. And Stalin's Russia was such an important battlefield for artists, writers, painters, film directors, and musicians. I could write a hundred thousand pages on Eisenstein alone. I've just finished a short biography of Isaac Babel (for Random House), and it was chilling to see how Stalin toyed with writers, large and small, forcing them to work within that curious and crazy mode of Socialist Realism, which was complete nonsense, and all the time in his heart of hearts he wanted them to write a book about him, to use their imagination to reinvent Joseph Stalin, but how could any of them have dared to do so? One or two might have tried, but as soon as they began to investigate his days as a bank robber and bandit in Batum, Stalin cut them off—the little father of his people couldn't afford to be seen as an ex-bandit. But how many dictators, after all, read Gogol and Isaac Babel and wanted to become a poet?

FT: Were the political arguments of Left and Right so current among our parents in the post-Second-World-War Bronx of our time part of your upbringing?

JC: Children of the Left and Right. Yes, of course, there was a Left and Right in the Bronx, swirling around Paul Robeson and the Rosenbergs. Robeson was attacked wherever he went. Robeson had been to Russia, Robeson won the Stalin Peace Prize. But my Paul Robeson had nothing to do with politics: the Robeson I remember sang "Ol' Man River," and he was as large and various and deep-throated as the Mississippi itself, more American than America. And the Rosenbergs, the Rosenbergs, how he religiously believed in their innocence, that J. Edgar and his stooges at the FBI had set them up, planted evidence, crucified them because they were Jews from the Bronx— at least it felt like the Bronx. And then to learn that for once in his life J. Edgar wasn't telling a lie, that Ethel and Julius really were spies. What a betrayal of our own past, of our own creed, as if we were little warriors in an army that went up in smoke—Tuten and Charyn who lived at the Loew's Paradise, who were rivals for life and for love, moving from politics to high art. Aren't we both bedraggled Don Quixotes fighting for rent control of the heart and mind, free candy bars for every kid on the block, ambulance patrol for our sick grandmas, and everything else that was incongruous in our crazy little world?

"Pinocchio Is Still Out There":
Listening to Jerome Charyn's
Everlasting Quest

Sophie Vallas/2009

This interview was conducted on 17 October 2009 and was never published. Printed by permission of Sophie Vallas.

SV: I'd like to start with the autobiographical dimension of your work. Some books can be easily classified as belonging to such a category, even if they are very different from each other, even if they play a lot with the genre: autobiographical novels such as *The Catfish Man* or *Pinocchio's Nose*, the recent autobiographical trilogy (*The Dark Lady from Belorusse*, *The Black Swan*, and *Bronx Boy*), and also shorter peritexts such as "Harvey" (1979), for instance, or the text you published in *The Contemporary Authors' Auto-biography Series* in 1984. And of course many other texts, such as the Isaac Sidel series, inspired by your brother.

JC: Yes, or even *Johnny One-Eye*, more precisely the essay I wrote at the end of the novel about how I fell in love with George Washington when I was a child. I think so much of your material comes out of your childhood. It almost seems to me that your self is formed by the age of six, and that very little happens afterwards. The contours of the family, the dynamics, the horrors, the frights are all there at a very early age and the music is there at an early, early age. This is where it seems to me it comes from, from the music.

SV: Do you have the impression, when you look back at your work, that it's essentially autobiographical? Is that the global vision of it that you have?

JC: Well, yes. For example my most recent novel that will be published in February, *The Secret Life of Emily Dickinson*, which is told through her voice. How could I enter her voice if I didn't feel that it was also my voice? The only way to really come to terms with it is that, I don't know, you cannibalize, or you somehow . . . I'm not talking about Emily Dickinson the poet, her poetry is incomparable, I'm talking about her *letters*, because that's what my novel started with. So many people said: "How did you have the nerve or the daring to write a novel in Emily Dickinson's voice?" Well, the answer is that it was my voice. Either I appropriated it, or I felt a closeness to her so that I could enter into it, or I wouldn't have been able to do it. There's no way you can do what you can't do; that's the whole thing. It worked because somehow there was a communion, or her music became my music, and we became one.

SV: It's quite close to what you did with Isaac Babel in *Savage Shorthand*.

JC: Yes, you see, one of the problems that came with that book is that, again, some critics would say, "How dare you compare yourself with Isaac Babel?" I wasn't *comparing* myself. I was just one writer looking at another writer and at Babel's work. Maybe I could have done a novel in Isaac Babel's voice, but I wasn't trying to do that. Now I'm thinking about doing a novel about Louise Brooks. Her story is just incredible. The question is: can I enter into the voice? The question is constantly the voice.

SV: It seems to be that it's even more than entering into the voice, for Babel. Reading the book, one has the impression that you've been carrying him inside all your life.

JC: Yes, exactly. He was a very, very important writer for me. His stories became critical for me. Yes, I have been carrying him inside. "What do you have to say about Isaac Babel?" some critics asked. Well, for me, it's not quite the same story. It's how I could open up Isaac Babel in terms of my own feelings. It's a love story, it's a love story addressed to Isaac Babel. Meeting Babel's daughter, Natalia, was a wonderful encounter. At first she was so suspicious of me—"What do you want? Why are you coming here?" And by the end, when she saw that I knew his work and that I was interested in literature, she changed from distrust to the opposite. That was a wonderful encounter and I needed to put it in the book. One of the difficulties is: how do you communicate the mystery of a writer? Because you know the rest of the work, you could read that book, but another reader coming to that book for the first time probably can't enter it in the same way.

SV: I think he can if he's sensitive to the fact that it is a love story between you and Babel. This is a very powerful way of entering into the story.

JC: I thought it was, I thought it was the way to do it. It didn't seem to work for most readers. And anyway, we don't know how things will be read in sixty years, or whether they'll be read at all. Language shifts so constantly that it's very hard to come to terms with what makes sense at a particular time and in a particular place.

SV: To go back to what the critics said about the book on Babel. Twenty years ago you said in an interview that when you wrote *The Catfish Man* or *Pinocchio's Nose* for instance, you took so much pleasure, and then the critical reactions were so negative that you were discouraged. People seemed to expect some kind of realism from you—which is completely beside the point, even in a book like *Savage Shorthand*.

JC: Well, it also seems to me . . . You're playing an instrument, trying to play like Glenn Gould, and they don't know what this instrument is. I find that most people don't understand language. You're working in different worlds, and there's nothing you can do. I have to play the instrument the way I know how to play it. My assistant once said, "Why don't you write a best-seller? Why don't you write a book that makes money?" And I said, "Well, I don't think I could. I would be unable to write it." [*Laughs*]. I think the writers who write best-sellers are doing the best they can. They're not fooling people. This is what they know and like to do. And it comes across. I wouldn't be able to do that.

SV: The Babel book is almost as much autobiographical as it is biographical.

JC: Yes, I think in a way all biography is autobiography. I felt very close to him, and I felt also very close to Emily Dickinson, particularly her use of language, in that it's so utterly unpredictable. There's no way you can predict how these images are going to come; they just come at you like stars, you know, like comets. I've never seen another writer like her, maybe Shakespeare at times. And I guess, it's difficult to say, but I need to feel the music or I can't read. I can't read most writers because I can't feel the music. When I read Cormac McCarthy, there's a music here, I can enter into it. When I read Nabokov—like "Lo-lee-ta: the tip of the tongue," I remember I think I was in high-school when I first saw those lines and I first heard the absolute music that he has.

SV: You also often mention the music of Faulkner and William Gass.

JC: Faulkner and Gass, and certainly James Joyce. Gass is to me an absolute marvel. "The Pedersen Kid" is wonderful.

SV: What about your other biographical essays, on Hemingway for instance, or on Marilyn Monroe? You rarely mention Hemingway in your interviews, when you talk about music for instance.

JC: Hemingway was the first writer that I discovered. When I read *The Sun Also Rises*, suddenly I was overwhelmed. Suddenly there was another world that I had not been able to grasp. It's only some of the stories and *The Sun Also Rises*. The rest of his work I don't like at all. The Nick Adams stories, the early stories. . . . What's interesting to me is how he formed himself as a writer, in Paris, just sitting there like a monk for two years, learning how to write; and then he became a parody of what he himself had discovered. It's very perverse and very strange. Perhaps if he had not been so successful, it wouldn't have happened. I don't know.

SV: Babel, Hemingway, even Marilyn Monroe—you like to write about those people who turned themselves into myths in order to hide their weaknesses.

JC: Yes. I'm very moved by Marilyn Monroe. I don't feel any affinity with Hemingway's life. I like the idea that he sat in Paris for two years learning how to write; that I do feel affinity for. But the rest . . . To me, he's a kind of travesty. Edmund Wilson wrote a wonderful essay, in 1937 or 1938, talking about his virtues and his great fallibility; he just fell in love with himself. You can't fall in love with yourself while you're writing. You have to be very, very modest it seems to me. I don't mean Nabokov, for instance, was a modest man; I mean he was modest in his writing. That's all I care about—what his life was is irrelevant. His work is that of a genius. It's just crazy, and wonderful, funny, perverse, strange. And I also wrote a novel on Jerzy Kosinsky. I just love the idea of the title of the novel, *Jerzy Kosinsky: A Novel*, because he's someone whose first few books I like very much. I don't like any of his later stuff, but both *The Painted Bird* and *Steps*, I think, are wonderful books. I wanted to write this novel. I admire writers, I have to say. I really admire the bravery, in a way, that Faulkner had—writing, at some point not even knowing if he was going to be published, and writing *The Sound and the Fury*. I love the sense of the absolute, the same absolute there is in "The Perdesen Kid." You have a man who's practically dying, destroying himself by writing.

SV: In one of your interviews you were asked a question about the intertext in your novels, and you said that, of course, literary intertexts were presences and voices in your work, but also it was your own "frightening face" that you contemplated in those intertexts. Could you expand on this?

JC: I think . . . I'm terrorized by everything except the writing itself, but I think the fright, the hysteria is still there, even in the writing. That's why the writing seems to skip, to move so quickly from image to image—the ghost of your self is almost within the text, the ghost of your own fright that you're getting away from. In writing you try to make yourself strong and yet, even while you're doing it, you're still the same little boy who's frightened of everything and who's trying to find some kind of wonder in the world. I would go back again to one's earliest childhood, where . . . I think we are formed very, very early. What those years mean, I don't know. I was always very, very independent. My mother said that as a child I never cried. When a child doesn't cry, what does it mean? That's very strange; it means that you're not able to articulate your own needs.

SV: Maybe crying is a language, and as you often explain in your interviews, and as is obvious in *The Dark Lady*, you were especially devoid of language, being the son of immigrants who didn't master English.

JC: Maybe, I don't know. I remember this image: I was perhaps six years old, we were in the country in one of these little places we went to, and my older brother was nine, and my mother was feeding him and I was eating by myself—what a strange image. He's nine years old and like a baby, she's feeding him, and I'm there, managing by myself. I was always alone. And the aloneness, I wouldn't say loneliness, but the aloneness of the writer is critical; you have to be alone. There's no other way that you can do it.

SV: You have to be alone, but as you said before, you have all those voices coming to you or "cannibalizing" you as you said or that *you* cannibalize—other writers, other musics.

JC: Yes, you're right. In that sense, the history of other works that you've read, whether it's Babel, or Faulkner, or James Joyce . . . For me, one has to respect a paragraph because the whiteness on the page is as important as the language. If you fill up the page with a ten-page paragraph, I find it unreadable; I just can't read it. I need the interspace. That's why the Gass text is so incredible: it's really about empty space, about snow that overwhelms you, and also the fact that it's the only text I've ever seen in which he doubts the existence, he doubts who we are, and what we are, what we might ever become. He doubts everything, and that's what makes the piece so strong. Did the Pedersen Kid really exist, did William Gass ever exist, did this language ever exist? It's just a remarkable text.

SV: To go back to this global vision of your work. Your very first texts, to me, start with a vision of the community, the Jewish community, language and humor, and then you seemed to move to the "I," to Jerome, Jerome the Catfish, Jerome Copernicus, Pinocchio.

JC. Yes, but it's also depending on what I write. The period when I wrote the first novels, I had read Hemingway, Faulkner—I don't know whether I'd read Nabokov at that point. So, I think I was writing out of what I thought I knew, the world that I knew, without really coming to terms with the power of the imagination and the ability to hallucinate oneself into another world and into another text. The novel I like best, which most people think is un-readable, is *Eisenhower, My Eisenhower*, because that's completely crazy; it's just all about language.

SV: Yes, you've often said that it's the novel in which you found your voice.

JC: Yes, I found who I was. Up to that point, with *On the Darkening Green* and *Once upon a Droshky*, it was a voice that was familiar to me, but after that, it was very difficult to assume a third-person narration. It was very, very hard to do. Now, to me it's interchangeable. For instance in the novel about Emily Dickinson I wrote both in the first and in the third persons, and I didn't feel any difficulty in switching from one to the other. But how to ap-propriate the third person was really a ten-year task. I didn't know how to do it. I didn't know how to make the third-person my own voice. That was very difficult.

SV: You started with stories about the community then you switched to much more personal texts, voices.

JC: But they still reflect the communities. If you look at *The Dark Lady*, the community is critical.

SV: That's what I meant, yes. It's another way of reaching the community through the "I." In 1995, while in the process of writing *The Dark Lady from Belorusse*, you gave an interview to Michel Lebrun and you said: "I feel less and less like a fabulist, and more and more like a trapper diving into his own past, looking for images, sounds, and smells." Do you remember what moti-vated such a new period in your writing?

JC: Well, I couldn't have written *The Dark Lady* until my mother died, be-cause it's very hard to write about your mother, and about your mother as a sexual person, but on the other hand, you're looking for images, for feelings, for looks, and people's faces that you can trap like a hunter, so you go back into the past like a hunter. Memory is merely hunting for details that you lost and that you have to find again. I feel I'm a hunter, sort of, I don't know how to say, swallowing my own past and regurgitating it and finding those images that work, and discarding those images that don't work. It's not really a memoir. It's finding a kind of shape that makes sense for you. I don't think it's ever changed, even from the moment I began writing. All you're doing is trying to find one particular detail that will tell you a story. The story is always in the detail, it's nothing more than that.

SV: After 1995, nevertheless, you seem to abandon more or less pure fiction, except for the occasional Isaac novel, and you publish either the autobiographical trilogy, or the biographical essays (on Babel, Hemingway, Marilyn, and soon on Joe DiMaggio), or what could be called fictional portraits, or again biographical novels.

JC: I wouldn't put it that way. While I was living in France, not hearing my language and sort of being away from my culture, you lose a kind of courage, you know, the courage of your own imagination. So in Paris, I really had to salvage my own past, as in *The Dark Lady*, or I had to go into another landscape, Isaac Babel's for instance. New York City still remained with me. In other words, while I was away from New York City, it was easier to write about New York City, but I didn't have the power to write a novel such as *The Green Lantern* or to really deal with a fictional world as in *Johnny One-Eye*. It was only when I really returned to New York, when I began coming back to New York more often, around 1997, when I became to live more and more in New York, that a little bit of my courage came back. It was amazing, I hadn't written a novel in a long time, and I sat down to write *The Green Lantern* and the music just . . . as if the music had hidden, waiting to come out. It's as if you're never in control of what you are. Certain things are blocked, certain things are killing you, and then suddenly everything opens up and you find your music—it's losing the music and finding it again. Once I began to move back to New York City and to live more and more in New York City, I returned to fiction a lot more.

SV: This fiction is very historical fiction: you focus on Stalin, or Benedict Arnold, or Emily Dickinson, or Jerzy Kosinsky in this novel which will come out soon.

JC: Yes, but for example, if you look at the book on Jerzy Kosinsky, it's not really different from *The Tar Baby*; it's *The Tar Baby* in the same way. So you see, your statement—I don't believe it is accurate in terms of any kind of change taking place. I was still able to write the Isaac Sidel novels because the music was still there, so if you move towards biographical novels, I would say that if I were younger, I would never been able to write the novel on Emily Dickinson. I wouldn't have found Emily Dickinson's voice. It's having the courage to find your language again that allowed me to enter her world. Now, if you ask why I don't write about more contemporary things, remember the fifteen years I was basically not living in New York. So what was I going to write about? I mean you're not listening to your music, to your language. I wasn't in New York during 9/11, you see. I didn't experience that, and current history doesn't have the same shape, doesn't have the same form. So if the question is, why don't I write a more contemporary novel, well, go back to my other novels—how contemporary were they? *The Franklin Scare* was about FDR. I don't see the change in the same way that you see the change. Maybe you're right though.

SV: In many of your texts, for instance *Johnny One-Eye* or *Savage Shorthand*, you include an explanatory peritext, either a preface or a postscript. In all those peritexts, you carefully link the books to your childhood.
JC: Yes, because they're really about me. I'm just using them to write about me. They're an excuse to talk about my love for Joe DiMaggio, or to talk about my love for Isaac Babel. I'm talking about a fan. I've always been a fan, even as a child. I was a fan of actors—it was Tyrone Powell when I was a kid, and when I got older it was Hitchcock or Tarantino as filmmakers. In the books you just mentioned, I was writing a fan's note to Isaac Babel or Joe DiMaggio. So few people understood that when they reviewed *Savage Shorthand*. They were unhappy because it wasn't the kind of traditional book. I'm not interested in that. I'm not a collector of details or information. I was just writing about why I loved Isaac Babel.

SV: So what you said in 1995 about diving into your own past applies to . . .
JC: To everything! To everything! To everything I write. Okay, when I wrote *Blue Eyes*, it was inspired by my brother who was a homicide detective, but it wasn't about my brother as a homicide detective. It was about a few details that I happened to notice when I went around with him. You're always looking for that one image. With Emily Dickinson it's the tattoo on Tom's arm that really motivates the entire book, and this is not a historical fact. There was no Tom and there was no tattoo. So you search for something that makes the book cohere inside your head. When I think about it, it's not

about Emily Dickinson at all, it's about me. About me as Emily Dickinson. How I would behave if I was a woman in the nineteenth century, in Emily Dickinson's skin, without her talent, but trying to be Emily Dickinson. That's it. So few people can deal with that. They say it's too daring, it's not accurate, it's not this, it's not that, but who cares? Finally you don't write for anybody except yourself. So, nothing really matters. You want the book to succeed, you want to have good reviews, you go on the radio. But what do the sales really mean? To me they really mean that the publisher won't make me crazy when I write my next book and will leave me alone. That's the only thing sales mean to me.

SV: I'd like you to say a few words about the text that you wrote about yourself in 1984, published in *Contemporary Authors' Autobiography Series*. I like the Isaac Babel sound of it. Were you contacted by the editors to write a text?

JC: Yes, they offered you a certain amount of money to write an autobiographical text. I did it in my own private way. You can only write something the way you can write it, so it came out as if it was some kind of fiction. Otherwise I wouldn't have been able to do it, you know. It was as much fiction as anything, just as the book on Babel is a work of fiction. It's not a Nabokovian text, because even though I love Nabokov and *Pale Fire*, I wasn't trying to imitate Nabokov. I was just writing a novel about Isaac Babel but it wasn't a novel. Which is the best thing to do, to remain somewhere in between two landscapes. If I had to write another autobiographical piece today it would be written in a form that makes sense for me today. It would have the music that I have at the moment. It's only about the music, either the music comes or not.

SV: You often use the metaphor of music—you're looking for the right music, you say, when you write or when you read. Do you listen to music when you write?

JC: No, I don't listen to music. I like classical music, I like jazz, but I don't know that much about music. To me it's the music of language. I'd say that of all writers today William Gass certainly has the best ear. Read his essay on the color blue. And Cormac McCarthy also has this wonderful sense of music. I don't know if the music of language can be compared with Beethoven, Stravinsky, or Mozart—I wouldn't know. I like jazz because I like the idea of improvisation.

SV: It's just that you mentioned Glenn Gould a few minutes ago, and I've always thought that your language sounds like *The Goldberg Variations.*
JC: Yes, I think you're right! I love the fact that Gould played on this little piano, leaning over. It was his own piano, his own instrument. And he couldn't perform in concerts.

SV: Yes, and he also suffered from some kind of difficulty to speak, and it's a theme which is omnipresent in your work. A lot of your characters suffer from aphasia, dyslexia, they have a very peculiar language and sometimes they have no language at all.
JC: Yes, the inability to master language is often a language in itself. Those are the people who move me, people who cannot speak. In a way, Emily Dickinson moves me because in some profound way she also couldn't speak, couldn't articulate who she was in her own time. Yes, you hit the point; really language is about no language. What I'm trying to do is make the unspeakable speak. That's the mission that I have. To find a voice for those who have no voice. What is their music? If you go back to one of my first stories, "Faigele, the Idiotke," it's exactly . . . her voice is trying to fly, and when of course she tries to fly she fails. This is a way of singing. She can't sing, so . . . It's always about attempting the impossible, and failing. There's a kind of suicide embedded in the text, also, because it's essentially about failure. It's never the text that you want it to be; perhaps the closest to where it might be would be the very last pages of *Emily Dickinson*, where suddenly she's singing about her own death, which is a form of suicide. She was so much ahead of her time that she didn't understand, to some degree, why she was suffering. She was so much more intelligent that anyone around her.

SV: It's very similar to Melville's own position at roughly the same time, isn't it? Melville, who is also omnipresent in your work?
JC: Yes, but Melville was a man, and it made all the difference. What could a woman do in 1850? She could become a wife, or she could become a spinster school-teacher. She couldn't be a lawyer, she couldn't be a doctor. She could teach in a school, get married or, in Emily's instance, she became a spinster. She wasn't very attractive. And yet, what a gift it is for us to have this poetry that comes out of a strange, profound way. The lack of her voice. She couldn't articulate who she was.

SV: Yes, that is something that is quite close to your own situation. When reading you, I often think of French writer Patrick Modiano. Although his novels are completely different from yours, you do have common points: for some historical reasons, his identity, and I think this is true for you too, was from the start extremely fragile, uncertain, blurred because of his parents' complex history. In both your works, also, we find the overwhelming presence of the historical context your parents experienced—the war, for him, and the period of the Occupation in Paris, and the conflicts in eastern Europe for you, and the issue of immigration.

JC: Yes, Modiano. I can read Flaubert, Baudelaire, and Rimbaud in French (those are the three French writers that formed me), but I'm not sure I could get Modiano in French, and it's so hard to translate.

SV: The question of his origins, and I think it holds true for you too, is at the origin of his whole work. Because his were so blurred and fragile, he's kept going back to them and dreaming them in a long-lost Paris. You often use the expressions "to mythologize," "the mythologization of one's life," but have you ever had any other choice, in fact? Because of your fragile and incomplete origins, could you do anything else but mythologize your own life?

JC: Probably not. I don't know what I could have done. I started as a painter and I didn't have any talent at all. I didn't have that much talent with words but somehow . . . Maybe it gave me a kind of pleasure. I don't know, but when I started writing, I can tell you, it wasn't much better. I think it's a very important question. I would say that no, I didn't have much of a choice. Could I have done it better? Did I screw up my life? In many aspects, yes. But on the other hand, pain is a very important lesson. When I first came to Paris, I wanted to live here, but as I said before, I lost my courage as a writer. That was the time when I was doing *The Dark Lady*. I was writing those books because these were the only books that I could write. I couldn't go into a larger landscape, I'd lost it. When I did *War Cries over Avenue C*, I realized I couldn't go any further as a novelist. I had taken the novel to where I could take it and the other side of that was insanity, unintelligibility. So I tried to move to "a more realistic" world with *Paradise Man*, but it's just as crazy, it's more realistic, but just as crazy—the world is crazy. Whatever I do, I will turn it into a mythology; I'll mythologize whatever I write. So in *Paradise Man*, Holden is a killer, but he's so much more than a killer. In *Darlin' Bill*, again, Bill is a *flingueur* [gunfighter], he kills with words.

SV: Are you interested in all the critical theories about fictions or narratives of the self, self-narratives or again autonarration?

JC: I'm interested in the theory, especially theory in cinema because this is what I teach. But I find that most theory in literature sort of pushes the writer to the side and makes the text . . . It's almost as if the text becomes the author, and the author isn't there, and I don't agree with that. Whatever I write, for instance the novel about Emily Dickinson, however you interpret it, it still comes from my own love of Emily Dickinson, no matter what is refracted in the text. Tell me what you think about those theories.

SV: Well today, a lot of theory is being written in France about what is called "autofiction," that tries to define this genre which is in-between life and literature, in-between real life and fiction. Do you make a clear difference in your mind between the autobiographical experimentations you made in the 1980s (*The Catfish Man, Pinocchio's Nose*) and the apparently more classical autobiographical volumes that you published recently (the Bronx trilogy)?
JC: I would say that there's a difference in landscapes. In the recent books, landscape, rather than expands, contracts. In *Pinocchio's Nose* you're looking at one end of the telescope, and in *The Dark Lady*, it's the other end of the telescope. But I still would have to go back to the sentence, and it seems to me that there is not that great a difference between writing fiction and nonfiction. You're still stuck with the sentence and the music of the sentence. Let's say with Marilyn Monroe, I wasn't writing a novel about her, but I don't see that much difference with writing fiction. I would say *Pinocchio's Nose* was outrageous and going everywhere and expanding the landscape. But I don't see any great difference. There are works that don't work. When I wrote *American Scrapbook*, I was rather unhappy, and I wasn't really able to expand it. The world was interesting but the language wasn't interesting, that was the problem. When you have the music, everything opens up; when you don't have the music, everything closes.

SV: How do you consider the paratexts that you've published, for instance this piece about your brother, entitled "Harvey," which was published first in France in 1979 and then in the U.S. in 1981?
JC: [*Looking at the text*] I don't really remember this text.

SV: You don't? It's such a beautiful text. A first draft of it appears, very suddenly and completely out of the blue, in one of the notebooks containing the manuscript of *Secret Isaac*, as if it was a pressing, autobiographical parenthesis in the very middle of the fiction, as if those lines had been irrepressible at that moment. Then you used them, with very little change, in this very beautiful text that you published in the French newspaper *Libération* in 1979—a way to make the debt you have towards your brother public, as well as your love for him, it seems to me. I know you've been asked this question already, but I've never really found a direct answer to it: what did your brother think of this text, and of the fact that you often explained that he was instrumental in the creation of Coen?

JC: Well, my brother is very bright but he's not literate, so I don't know what he's capable of understanding. There's a love between us, but we're so divided politically, you know, sometimes it's difficult to talk to him. He was critical for me in that, as a child, he saved my mind; he was the buffer between this crazy father of mine who, without even being conscious of it, wanted to destroy me, and me. So he was the substitute father; he was the father friend who could at least take me a little bit to where I had to go. Without him, I don't know what I . . .

SV: At one point in "Harvey" you write: "I want this primordial family when I'm Harvey's kid brother and nothing, nothing can come between us."

JC: Yes, because I felt very strong walking with my brother. He was very generous, sometimes sharing his friends with me. He liked me, he took care of me. It doesn't mean that Harvey wasn't mean at some point, but when he was younger he wasn't really. I remember the most magical moment of my life: it was Christmas and we had been given a gift, you know, one of these guns that shoot images on the screen, and on the screen there was this Christmas story, and it was so magical.

SV: "Harvey," as well as many other paratexts, peritexts, or interviews, are like lovesongs addressed to your brother, aren't they? Was it difficult for you to make such texts public? To be that open about your link to your brother?

JC: No, I don't think so. [*Thoughtful*] I think you're right, they *are* lovesongs to my brother; all the Isaac Sidel novels to some degree are lovesongs to him. I don't think he'll ever understand what our relationship was because he's much too conventional, you see, he lives in a much more conventional world. He won't see the connection, he probably won't. But basically what you discover is that the aloneness of the writer is essential. And even though what you have here is the voice of Harvey in my head, it's not Harvey. You have the voice of him which is not him, which is different.

I don't mind being alone, you see. I'm especially lonely in Paris because of the language. But in New York I'm not lonely for five minutes. I work very long hours here in Paris; I have to get out because I feel in some sense imprisoned. I'm always worried about something breaking, whereas in New

York, if it's broken, I call somebody up and they fix it. Here, I don't know how to negotiate [*laughs*]. But on the other hand I think coming to Paris was a critical step—whether it was the wrong step or the right step I don't know, but it was critical. In Paris . . . I was living with a woman for a long time and it didn't work out. I was willing to get married and have a child, but it didn't happen. This is the step I took. I love Europe, it didn't have to be Paris. As I knew some French, it was easier, and as I had some kind of recognition, it was easier for me to come here. I don't like America. I love New York. To me it's a European city, a city that came out of the old world; at least the New York *I* know was built out of the same immigration of Jews, of Italians, and Irish coming, you know, and so it's very, very familiar to me. But I paid a price. I don't say this in a sentimental way; I don't even know who I am or what my needs are. I know that when I sit down and I'm not frightened, the music will come. But that's all I know, I don't know what these texts mean, I don't know whether they'll please anyone. For the Emily Dickinson novel, I know it was important for me to write and to write her life. It was as if I was retelling her life from my point of view.

SV: In an interview, you were speaking about the Bronx and you said that today, the streets on which you grew up have disappeared, and the buildings also.
JC: Some of them, not all of them.

SV: Some of them, yes. I read an interview of Don DeLillo, about *Underworld* and about the way memory functions, one of the themes of the book. He was talking about this nostalgic return into the past and he said, "That's what I was doing: I was thinking backwards to the Bronx." Speaking about Nick, the hero of the novel, he added that he resembles this character: "It's not until he has a firmer sense of the wider culture and of the language necessary to enable him to enter that culture that he begins to feel the confidence to approach the world . . . What a writer does—a writer from a certain background—is write himself out of his neighborhood and into a broader culture. This is what Nick does [. . .] To a degree, this is what I did, you know, this is how I wrote myself out of the Bronx and into America." DeLillo and you have the same kind of background, a Jewish neighborhood and an Italian neighborhood in the Bronx. But your link with the Bronx is very different from his, isn't it?
JC: Yes, in fact he says the exact opposite of what I could say. My feeling was to write my way *into* the Bronx in order to take what was so destructive.

What he says is the exact opposite of what I wanted to do. I wanted to go back and deeper into the Bronx.

SV: But in a way you've never left the Bronx, have you?
JC: No, I don't think I have. I often go back to it and I always have a great time. I know DeLillo, but we've never talked about that. That would be a good point of discussion. His music is based on a kind of amnesia, and mine is the opposite.

SV: And the impression I have is that, mentally, you've never left the Bronx, so you don't really have to go back to it. You are still there.
JC: I have never wanted to leave the Bronx. The Bronx of my childhood doesn't exist anymore; it's now inside my head.

SV: When DeLillo says he wrote himself out of the Bronx to enter America, this sentence makes sense to me when I read his novels because of this political interest he has in American history. You too are very interested in history, but it's always through the prism of the Bronx.
JC: Yes, I am. I'm appropriating, cannibalizing history. Mine is the exact opposite of his. I realize that whatever it was, the imagination I had came from the Bronx because there was nothing there. The music comes from the absence of music. Adversity sometimes can be a kind of gift. It was a tremendous gift for me.

SV: In "An Interior Journey into the Belly of the Beast," you say at one point, speaking about the Bronx, that the mythology is always truer than the real facts. To me this sentence echoes a sentence in *Moby Dick*: "It's not down on any map; true places never are."
JC: Melville is a writer that I really, really admire.

SV: He's omnipresent in your books.
JC: The courage, the audacity, the loneliness, the madness . . . Leslie Fiedler wrote this wonderful essay about Melville's thunder; he is the one person who said no to this rampant American culture in the nineteenth century, and it wasn't recognized until the twentieth century. He's a writer who is literally reborn. He was not only forgotten during his life but people would think he was already dead. He was reborn as a writer in the 1920s or so, in the same way that Emily Dickinson emerged. These are the great writers of the nineteenth century. I suppose you would have to include Hawthorne,

but I don't have the same affection for him. They were working in an incredible isolation. Melville's genius in relation to the nothingness around him
was amazing.

SV: Could you write a book about Melville? Find the voice?
JC: No, I don't think I could write a novel about him.

SV: He's so present in your work.
JC: Yes, but . . . Maybe I could do it in the third person, but I couldn't do it
in the first person. There's a wonderful book by an Irish-American writer
called *The Master*, about Henry James. It's an incredible book. [*Laughs*] You
know, I have a strange relationship with Henry James. I love him, but I also
hate him because he's such a snob, and he only writes about the aristocracy,
and to me, his sympathies are on the head of a pin. He's a great, great writer;
I'm not taking anything away from him. The one piece I really love is "The
Beast in the Jungle," it's so autobiographical. But he's anti-Semitic in a terrible, terrible way, and he was such a snob! I never thought that either Melville
or Emily Dickinson were snobs. I felt that they encompassed . . . they were
larger than their surroundings. One could say that Henry James discovered
the modern novel, but I would much rather read Nabokov. Nabokov's sense
of parody, the sense of tearing down, I mean. James has satire but he has no
parody. He cannot really laugh at himself, whereas Nabokov really can. You
can see he's constantly making fun of himself. I don't really like Saul Bellow,
for instance, because to me he was regressive as a writer; he became more
and more conventional. Nabokov, on the contrary, became more and more
outrageous. I don't like *Ada* (I find *Ada* unbelievably boring), but I like everything else.

SV: I'd like to move on to the question of language. Did you speak Yiddish
when you were a child?
JC: I studied Yiddish at school but I didn't speak Yiddish with my parents.
We spoke English. I knew Yiddish because I studied it and because they
spoke Yiddish with each other, but they didn't speak Yiddish with us. I never
spoke Yiddish with them.

SV: So your mother tongue is English.
JC: . . .

SV: A strange English maybe?

JC: Yes. The word strange has to be added here, because the basic speakers that I had as a child are speakers who didn't really know English. My mother could speak Russian, my father could speak Polish. I studied Russian for a while. I would say "strange English," yes. It was certainly not the language of writers. I would say that this first English still sings in my work, I mean I sing for myself. I'm a comic writer; I believe in comedy, you know, in making people laugh, but at the same time my novels are all very sad books. There's an incredible sadness. That's a kind of contradiction, and yet . . . I love to laugh. That's why I love *Lolita*, I mean, it's so funny.

SV: It's very tempting to see you as someone who is always in-between languages—the English you spoke when you were young, this "strange English" with so many influences in it, and then there is the English of the Bronx.
JC: And also the English of school; it's almost as if I was learning a foreign language. The most important change of getting out of the Bronx and going to high school was that, for the first time, I encountered a middle-class culture of people who were reading books. I remember when I was in high school, Salinger was publishing his stories in the *New Yorker*, and it seemed so exciting. People were all reading him, and I read it too. I like Salinger's stories very much because they capture a certain time. I don't like *Catcher in the Rye*—I think it's a lot of bullshit—but the short stories . . .

SV: Isn't it also because of the children in these stories? The children in Salinger's short stories sometimes look and sound like yours. They are sometimes affected by those strange language diseases, and they're bright also.
JC: Yes! Yes, the children are so much more powerful than the adults, and also he captures the time. In "Uncle Wiggily in Connecticut," these women are talking about a very strange love affair, but so much in it is based on the war. Then I read that Salinger had met Hemingway in Paris. I guess he liked Hemingway. It's difficult for me to say what the influence is, but certainly I feel very, very close to "The Laughing Man" for example. I feel very close to those stories.

SV: In a letter that Joyce Carol Oates sent you in 1987, she mentions the "Metropolis Party" organized for the publication of the book, where she met "your mythic parents!" What did she mean by "your mythic parents," in your opinion? Did you have such an expression in mind when you wrote *The Dark Lady*, for instance?
JC: What I wanted to do with *The Dark Lady* . . . In *The Dark Lady*, I wanted

to give my mother a life that she should have had and never had. I wanted to make her into a heroine who was much larger than the background that she had and, also, the relation between both of us. She was beautiful, but she never used that beauty. I wanted her to be beautiful. In the opening sentence when everyone is looking at her, going up and down this hill . . . It took me a long time to write that sentence; that was a very hard book to write, because it was a different voice. Later on, with *The Black Swan* and *Bronx Boy*, that's a more familiar voice, but in *The Dark Lady*, if you've noticed, it's a very distant voice, almost as if it were in a picture frame. And that's because . . . how difficult it is to write about your mother having lovers, your mother as a sexual creature, you know. A boy can't, but you can do it if you put it inside a picture frame. In some sense, I censored the music; I was censoring my own music when writing it.

SV: The reader has the impression that you're looking at your mother from the point of view of the child you were at that time, but once again, it's a very special character, both childish and very mature.
JC: I'm not that child, you see. I'm reinventing myself. Whereas in *The Black Swan* and *Bronx Boy*, that's closer to the person that I was at the time because I am no longer writing about my mother. When you're writing about your mother, you have to be very wary, very careful. I was very much on my guard, you know. It was undoubtedly the most difficult book for me to write because there was such pain and such sadness that I was turning myself into . . . Remember, I was not literate at all as a boy, and this boy is very literate. This boy has a voice, a language. I wasn't that creature at all. I was really mythologizing my mother, making her larger than the background that she had. This is the life I wanted to give her, that she didn't have. In the book, she's in love with someone else. To do that, one could say that it's a violation, but I wanted my mother to have the life that she didn't have.

SV: You decided to include family photographs in the volume.
JC: Yes, because my mother is fantasized and real at the same time, so it was very important to me as a writer to show you an actual image of *The Dark Lady*. I happened to have those photographs, and it was important for me to use them to include the historical figure. But they're not really countertexts; I don't see anything as powerful as the sentences. I worked for six months on that first sentence, where the boy goes up the hill and down the hill in the same sentence, and the French translator said he couldn't translate it in one single sentence. It was too difficult; he had to do it in two sentences. To

me, the first sentences are always . . . they take you into the text, they take you onto the voyage, and the voyage is in the imagery of the words, not in the photographs.

SV: Your father is very absent from this book, and you show yourself as a boy who is in love with his mother's lovers.
JC: Yes, of course! [*Laughs*] That would make sense because I didn't recognize my father as my father. In the book, in a way, he's invisible, he doesn't really exist.

SV: Your ex-wife once wrote a poem about your mother and it finishes with the following lines, which she places in your mother's mouth: "'I know, dear,' you said flatly/ pain and disbelief dimming your Yiddish lilt/ 'I know. Jerome is a closed book.'" What do you think of this definition of you by your mother?
JC: [*Laughing out loud*] Did you find this text in the papers I gave to the Fales Library?! I didn't remember that poem! [*Reading* it] Actually it's not a bad poem! "A closed book," yes, because she had infinite power over me, but without *real* power. So I was always a closed book to her. I didn't tell her anything, so I was a closed book. I think in a way she loved me too much and she didn't know quite what to do with it. She was shocked because she said my brother always cried, and as I said before I never cried, and therefore she really didn't know how to take care of me, so we were almost like . . .

SV: . . . a couple?
JC: A couple! Yes, exactly. From the very beginning we were a couple. And she couldn't deal with it, she didn't know what it meant, she didn't understand.

SV: You wrote the three books of what I would call the Bronx trilogy after the death of your parents. Do you think you could have written them before?
JC: No. Maybe the second one, but not the first one. It was my way of mourning. As much as I loved my mother, I never told her I loved her. We had a very strange relationship. I married a woman who was not Jewish and my mother wouldn't come to the wedding, which was bad enough, but she blamed it on my father, and she didn't allow my brothers to go either, and I thought, "OK that's pretty awful." And then, when I took my wife to visit her, she had my younger brother take these phony wedding pictures, as if she was in fact involved in the wedding—that's what my ex-wife's poem alludes

to. I don't know why I allowed her to do that. It was all so stressful. Your mother should come to your wedding, no matter who you marry.

SV: In one of your interviews with Frederic Tuten, you said that for a long time you were very angry at your mother.
JC: Yes I was very angry, because there was a kind of fraudulence. Well, she did what she could. She always supported the idea that I wanted to become a writer, and she always supported what I wanted to do, and at the end of her life she gave me some money. I was about to go to Europe. They didn't have money. I shouldn't have taken it, but I did. It is very distressing to feel that you're stealing from your parents. They gave it to me, but . . .

SV: Was writing about her a way of paying it back?
JC: Well, I see it more as a way of giving her a kind of strength. I wouldn't want to have done a realistic portrait. I was thinking more of *The Portrait of the Artist*, you know, that kind of reinvention of oneself. In other words, you don't exist, and by writing it, you pretend that you do exist, you know, that you're a real person. I always feel very ambiguous about who I am, but once it's on the page, it's no longer ambiguous. I wouldn't have written *The Dark Lady* except that one of my French publishers, Gallimard, had a collection called "Haute Enfance" and they wanted a book. I realize that much of what I write depends on my relationship to some French publishers. You know, I did this book on table-tennis, and I wouldn't have done that if it hadn't been for the French publisher. It changed what I wrote. Going back to your question, I wanted to give my family a kind of legitimacy, I mean, not to make them a kind of royalty without being royal. By giving them life you make them royal. And of course I've also dealt with my older brother that way too. And I like him; I like him as a character.

SV: In the Isaac Sidel series, what I find fascinating is this confusion between father-figures and brother-figures. In one of your interviews you once said about Isaac: "He was an evil father-figure in the beginning, then a brother, then I grew and he grew older. He's not an alter ego, not a double, but he cannibalized me and I cannibalized him, and at some point we came together."
JC: I think that's very well said! [*Laughs*] I'm not sure I'd be able to articulate it that well today!

SV: Coen is an image of Harvey but also a mixture of Harvey and you, as you said, and Isaac, the father-figure, is responsible for Coen's death and spends his life paying for it. In this saga, you seem to have merged your father, Harvey, and yourself into those characters.

JC: Yes, yes, and also Isaac is constantly finding another son, other Coens, and then there's his daughter, Marilyn, who doesn't call him dad because Marilyn is in love with him.

SV: In the same interview you also said: "Fathers multiply, they are their own sons." There is no longer that verticality of different generations, of fathers and sons—everything becomes confused.

JC: Yes, everything is transmogrified, and everything is confused, and all stories are one story. It's all the same. Isaac is going to pay for his entire life for killing Coen, and he's always going to find other Coens to take Coen's place, and he will dream of killing them. It's something that John Malkovich said when I met him. He wanted to do one of my plays and we were talking about cruelty, and I guess he must have had an older brother who wasn't nice to him. I don't know exactly, I don't know his biography, but he was very right when he said that cruelty could also be very tender, and that was an observation I wouldn't have had on my own. It *can* be tender. I don't know why but I'm constantly drawn to assassins. Coen is a killer too . . .

SV: . . . "with sad eyes," as you often said.

JC: Yes. And Holden in *Paradise Man*, and this character in this new novel I'm writing about Berlin. They're sons looking for something that they can never find.

SV: Very often also, in your books, there are historical father-figures, Mussolini, Stalin, and they are like ogres devouring their own children.

JC: Yes, like "Saturn Devouring his Son," the Goya painting, which is a very important influence in my writing. I've seen it in the Prado. This Berlin novel, it opens in the Prado when this character strangles a diplomat. He's part of the German secret service and he's haunted by this image of Saturn devouring his son, and he becomes confused. He thinks it's the son devouring the father. The father devouring the son is also the son devouring the father. And anyway, writing about the Jews in Theresienstadt, you know the concentration camp, one comes to the conclusion that the victims have a tremendous power over the victimizers. The victimizers are hypnotized by the victims in some strange way. It's very frightening and disturbing.

SV: But on the whole, the reader, as well as you, feels tenderness for Isaac. He's a rather positive father-figure, in spite of all he does.

JC: Yes and also, there is a kind of morality to what he does. He never does it for personal gain. He doesn't have a penny in his pocket. He's doing it out of some kind of crazy . . . He's larger than morality itself; he makes his own morality. What happens to the story after the writer stops writing? The story still continues in some way. At some point, you don't need the author anymore. The world of Isaac is out there. You can continue with the characters, think of other adventures.

SV: In a text about Melville's "Bartleby," Gilles Deleuze suggests that American literature in the nineteenth century broke away from the British novel by rejecting the father-figure and substituting the ideal of a universal fraternity, brotherhood, which develops on the very ruins of the paternal function. Brothers are extremely present in your books, not just Harvey, but for instance Paul Morphy, the Bartlebys, Hernando and the gang of muchachos in *The Catfish Man*, or the cellar rats and Basil Roth in the Bronx Trilogy. Your work is full of those bands of brothers, brothers multiplying everywhere.

JC: Yes, brothers multiply just as language multiplies. To go back to Deleuze: What happened in the American novel, with Melville the first one and maybe Emily Dickinson the second one, was that the music was very different because it was no longer a class society. These bands of brothers mean that we're all anonymous, we're all classless.

SV: Interchangeable?

JC: Interchangeable, yes. Certainly in *The Confidence Man*. Appearances are everything; there's nothing more than the masks. It's a novel that's so contemporary.

SV: But there are two periods in Melville's work, up to *Pierre* and afterwards, after this terrible disillusion. In the first period, in *Moby Dick* for instance, this ideal of brotherhood is still very naïve.

JC: Yes, and sexual too. There's a tremendous kind of homosexuality implied in the relationships between the sailors. The feeling in Melville for the first time is that all men are brothers, and you cannot have a class system when men are brothers. And this is his power. Even if you wanted to see the ship as the ship of capitalism in *Moby Dick*, on the other hand, it's also a ship of brothers. What is also so contemporary about Melville is this deep sadness about capitalism that's coming back to haunt us. The individual is displaced. Where's the individual when the commodity takes over? Finally there's no place. We've seen this in the arts, we've seen this in books. When the book becomes mass-produced rather than something that's odd and unusual, it has to be a commodity like every other commodity. Books are too eccentric. If you don't have any Melville or the possibility of a Melville, you don't have the possibility of writers. That's what's disappearing.

SV: In the papers you gave to the Fales Library I came across documents that you used for *The Catfish Man*, on Paul Morphy and idiot savants. You seem to have been fascinated by such characters at the time.
JC: Yes, and also progeria, the idea that you're an old man even before you're young. Even if people didn't like it, I loved the film about Benjamin Button, because it was such an incredible concept. It went on too long, you shouldn't have seen him as a baby at the end. The film should have ended much earlier. I've always felt, and that's a conceit because it's not true, that the film writer had read my work! It almost seemed as if I had written it. It's very close to my work, the imagination.

SV: To go back to those brothers, those little brothers in your work who are suffering kids, because they can't speak or because they are somehow too bright for the world they live in: In an article Pierre-Yves Pétillon mentions a conversation he had with you, and your interest in Wittgenstein and in aphasia. Do those characters that keep popping up on your books have a link with your silent childhood, and to your silent father?
JC: Well, that's difficult to say. I think they are definitely linked to *my* silence, but maybe it's my father's silence, I don't know. Maybe I had a greater affection for him than I'm willing to admit.

SV: What about your younger brother, Marvey?
JC: I like him, but he doesn't seem to enter into the mythology in the same way. Maybe I'm sort of pushing him out, I don't know. I've never felt close to him. I certainly wasn't nice to him, I don't mean I was mean but I was . . . Maybe what bothered me was that I saw my father's affection for him when he was a baby. I haven't thought about it in years, but how tender he was with him, how untender he was with me. Why did he dislike *me* so much?

SV: You never asked him?

JC: I don't think he could have answered. I just think it's because my mother loved me. I don't know how a baby knows that. I'm the baby who never cried. I've seen his tenderness towards others. What went wrong? I don't know what went wrong.

SV: As I suggested before, the piece that was published in *Contemporary Authors Autobiography Series*, to me, sounds like Babel's faked autobiography which you discuss in *Savage Shorthand*, a text which he entirely forged. Did you have this Babel text in mind when you wrote yours? There are a lot of autobiographical elements, of course, which are to be found in your books, but . . .
JC: It's also a forgery.

SV: In this text your father is in the foreground and your mother almost invisible. There's this part in which you meet your father at the end of the text and he says, "I'm the only theme you've ever had."
JC: [*laughing*] Yes, I remember!

SV: And then he says that "Your work is one long slap at your dad." Do you still have this impression?
JC: [*laughing*] No, no. When he's saying that, it's myself saying that to myself. It's giving him a place that he didn't really have, you know. It's funny, I remember that now.

SV: Is he the only theme, or one of the major themes you've ever had?
JC: I don't think so. I think the search for the father is, but it's the absence of him and the need to find . . . And it's also throughout Melville, this search of the father.

SV: In the same text, you use the image of Pinocchio.
JC: Yes. Pinocchio was very, very important to me. The two books I read first were *Bambi* and *Pinocchio*, and I was overwhelmed. It was so frightening when Bambi's mother dies, and when Pinocchio is in the Land of Toys. That's how I discovered writing. I couldn't believe how powerful those stories were.

SV: When you evoke Pinocchio in this text, there is a long paragraph about literary influences, who is the master and who is Pinocchio, and this part comes just after the part about your father. The father-figure therefore superimposes with the shadows of the literary masters. When I read it, I thought of *The Invention of Solitude*, in which Paul Auster also uses Pinocchio.

JC: A wonderful book.

SV: It's also a book about an absent father, a father whose eyes are unable to watch the son, a book about the quest for the father, about being a son, finding one's place as a son, as a writer.

JC: It's done with such acute observation, such humility. The second half of the book isn't as good as the first. The first story of *The Man Who Grew Younger*, "1944," starts with Pinocchio. That was a very autobiographical work, with my brother, and . . . What I was trying to do . . . I was trying to find a music for a musicless world. To find the music that wasn't there. My background was a dead-end, a terrifying place. It had no language, no understanding of art. I don't know how to say it.

SV: Pinocchio is the epitome of the lost, abandoned child who has to give birth to himself.

JC: Yes. I had to give birth to myself as a writer. I couldn't give birth to myself as a man. I didn't succeed. I had too many doubts; I was never able to have a long, powerful, tender relationship with a woman. It never seemed to work out. But I could give birth to myself as a writer. That I had the power to do. Not having a language I had to give myself a language.

SV: What Auster says in *The Invention of Solitude* about Pinocchio having to save his father from the shark in order to become a real boy—he uses Kierkegaard. Does it make sense to you?

JC: It does make sense except that Geppetto isn't his father. He doesn't have a father. So this idea of fathering Pinocchio is already sentimental. He was manufactured. He has a stepfather.

SV: But when Geppetto makes the wooden boy, there is also this dream of making a child without a mother.

JC: Yes, I agree to that, but the terror of Pinocchio, from my point of view, is that he has no father. Geppetto, okay, it works because Geppetto has no sexuality, he doesn't have to be afraid of him. A father without sexuality is a father who's never going to threaten you. So in that sense, I saw Geppetto as his creator, but not as a father. In *Pinocchio's Nose*, Mussolini is the real father. In *Johnny One-Eye*, Washington is the father. It's the eternal quest for the father. Pinocchio's quest is also finding the father. Not that I disagree with what Auster says; I just don't see it that way.

SV: Well, it's linked to this relationship Auster had with his father and the idea that he has to build this memorial of words after his father's death.
JC: Well, one has to try to imagine—and I don't know anything about Paul Auster—that his father was also a man of words. I don't believe he was an immigrant; it seems that he was well-educated.

SV: His father was a real estate agent, if I remember correctly. There is this scene in *The Invention of Solitude* when his father goes and sees him in Paris, and he tells him that he went to a library to read his poems; and Auster imagines his father sitting in this library with his coat on, not understanding a word of what he reads. I don't think his father was a man of words. The text says that "it made no sense for him to have a poet as a son." There was a misunderstanding between the father and son.
JC: Yes, but one could always say that for a real estate agent, numbers are words. It is a language. He had a language. My father didn't. I didn't want Geppetto to be my father. I wanted Mussolini. I wanted a man of power!

SV: Pinocchio, at the same time, can be seen as a child going through terrible mistreatments: He nearly dies; he has his feet burnt; even the blue fairy threatens him in terrible ways; he's swallowed by a shark. Psychoanalytical interpretations of the tale insist on the fact that it's a story on abusing parents, not just the father, and a story about what a child has to go through, even in his parents' hands, in order to survive.
JC: Yes, I don't disagree with that. And yet, first and foremost, it's an invented story. It's Pinocchio, the wooden boy going out into the world, getting his feet burnt, discovering the world's assassin—what an obscene word, ass-ass-in. I was overwhelmed by that word when I read Pinocchio for the first time! It stuck with me, the word assassin. I guess the Pinocchio that I was is not the Pinocchio Paul Auster was. I saw myself as the fatherless child trying to manufacture the quest, my quest. Pinocchio's quest is to become human, you know. My quest was to find a father. What does that mean? Not being able to find my father, I became my own father. But becoming your own father, you pay a tremendous price, it seems to me, in terms of disconnection with the world. If you are your own father you are your own creator, and in some sense you exist outside the world. And also in a very obvious sense, in an immigrant world, the child becomes the father to the parents. I used

to write the letters and pay the bills of my parents. I remember I needed a recommendation for Columbia University and I went to this place where my father manufactured slippers, and I asked him a letter of recommendation. But he was illiterate, and I had to write a recommendation for myself. I had to write my own recommendation. The idea of the quest for this common language which an average middle-class kid never has, because your parents have no language, even at school it's difficult, it's still a negotiation. For me, it was essential, it was one essential quest to master a language because without it I had nothing. And I'm not even sure I mastered it, but at least, I was able to go to Columbia University, which was not that easy to get into.

SV: Thanks to grants?

JC: I had a state scholarship. It was not expensive; the tuition was only five hundred dollars. I had a full scholarship for NYU, but I didn't take it because I knew that Columbia was a better school. I made decisions which never made economic sense, because I had a full scholarship to NYU, but it made sense psychologically. I wasn't sure that NYU could give me the power that I needed. I remember, the first year, I was in a literary magazine, and I wanted to become part of that world, but I realized that the editors were so condescending that I worried that they would discourage me to such a degree that I wouldn't want to go on writing. Maybe I was being too defensive, because I should have joined the magazine. It's very helpful, but I didn't have the confidence.

SV: Were your parents proud when you went to Columbia?

JC: I think they were, and even my father gave me some money. I was very startled, because he didn't have a lot of money. He was a strange person. I remember that he read a review of *The Man Who Grew Younger*, and it wasn't a complimentary review because it said I was making fun of Jews or whatever, and he started to cry. He said, "Look what they're saying about my son." So you see, he did have the feelings, but his anger and jealousy were so intense that he didn't really know how to deal with them.

SV: Pierre-Yves Petillon once analyzed the passage in *The Catfish Man* in which you evoke your father playing his violin, and he says this violin has never left your mind, just like the voice of your father.

JC: Yes, he's right. Marc Chénetier once said that my characters are always dancing into a room, there always a physical movement as if music was playing.

SV: Is this music coming from your father's violin still painful to you?

JC: No, I think I've come to terms with the Bronx. It's not painful to go there; I like to go there. Did you see the piece I wrote for the *Washington Post* about growing up in the Bronx? I think in a sense, I never could have been a writer if I had not been defined by that absence. My writing came from the definition of absence, from being Pinocchio without a father, from being a wooden boy without words, and the quest to discover the father and language at the same time. I'm not sure I would have been driven to words if I'd had a middle-class background. They meant so much to me, that there was little else that mattered. And also to master something doesn't necessarily mean that you have to succeed. To master something is a very personal quest, but if you ask me whether I've mastered my language I would say well, I don't know, I'm still trying, and maybe I haven't. While you're working, what's exciting about any kind of writing is that you're discovering things that you never knew before. Imagination is so . . . Could I have written the book about Emily Dickinson twelve years ago? Probably not. I wouldn't have had the confidence. I think you need an incredible amount of confidence to say that you can do something. Could I write about Nazi Berlin? I don't know. I certainly tried; I didn't feel frightened while doing it. And this concentration camp was also "charynesque" in that it was a phony concentration camp, it was like a movie set, it's where the Germans had the Red Cross come to see, it was called "the City that Hitler built for the Jews," and it was the lie that Hitler was the great father who was treating his Jews with respect. What a strange, perverse place to set part of a novel in. It's a phantom. I mean, okay, a concentration camp is a killing field. People weren't killed in Theriesenstaadt. They were maybe sent from there to Auschwitz, but they weren't killed there. This is where Jews were supposed to live out their retirement, a fantasy, so it was like a movie set, with a fake café.

SV: It sounds like what you develop in *Savage Shorthand*, when Babel is sent to a camp, and all those lies begin to develop about the great life he was supposed to have there.

JC: Yes. To me, Theriensenstaadt was something I could write about. I couldn't write about Auschwitz, I just couldn't. I wouldn't want to. When I discovered Theresienstaadt—and the nickname they had for it was paradise; this was the paradise that Jews were going to be sent to—I thought, well . . . I had originally taken the characters to America, but it didn't work. I couldn't create a world there. It just didn't have any power, so I had to go back, and rewrite what I had.

I seek the ultimate. I seek to do the undoable even though you know you can't do it. I seek the perfect world. I wanted to write a novel by Emily Dickinson that could have been by Emily Dickinson. Of course, you're going to fail, but so what?

SV: Gilles Deleuze once quoted Proust: "Beautiful books are written in some kind of foreign language," and I think it casts a very strange light on your work. To me, you write in a foreign language. And sometimes you use foreign voices such as Babel's, or Emily Dickinson's, other voices that you make yours, or into which you slip your own words.

JC: Yes, when you write you are writing in a foreign language in some sense. But there again, it's very, very perverse. If you asked me what I've done, I'd say I've done nothing. I'm just warming up, just trying to get where I have to go. Where do I want to go, I don't know, but that's the quest. Pinocchio is still out there, finding his adventures and looking for new adventures. Okay, maybe he's going to get his feet burnt again, but he's still out there. To me, writing a book is the greatest adventure in my life. I'm Pinocchio. When it doesn't work out, the adventure fails, but on the other hand, it's very exciting to invent. I don't know today what I'm going to write tomorrow. I have some kind of notion in my head, but I don't know where I'm going to go. Even though I've finished the first draft, I'm going to rewrite it. I don't know whether this section on Theresienstadt works. I'll have to read it and see. But I know it was the right place to go. Either you have a sense of form or you don't, and I think I do have it. The architecture is invisible but the structure is there. Form is everything. I always feel that writing is like sculpting, what you do is getting rid of what's not essential.

Finding the Music:
An Interview with Jerome Charyn on
The Secret Life of Emily Dickinson

Richard Phelan and Sophie Vallas / 2011

From *E-rea* (*Revue électronique d'études sur le monde anglophone*) 8/2 (2011). © *E-rea*. All rights reserved. *E-rea* can be viewed at www.erea.revues.org. Reprinted by permission of Sylvie Mathé.

SV: Recently, you seem to have moved to nonfiction more and more. In a few interviews, you said that from the moment when you decided to write about your mother in *The Dark Lady from Belorusse*, you were more and more interested in writing nonfiction; although as you often underline it, it's not that easy to distinguish between fiction and nonfiction.

JC: Well I write nonfiction in a very particular way. It's fictionalized nonfiction. I've just finished a book on the baseball player Joe DiMaggio, which again is a very personal book. You try to do it in a way that no one else could do it, you know; you personalize it. It doesn't mean it's better, I'm not saying that, I mean it's . . .

SV: It's yours.
JC: Yes, you leave your imprint on it.

SV: *Savage Shorthand: The Life and Death of Isaac Babel* was published in 2005. It is a biographical essay, but it's also autobiographical.
JC: It's an autobiographical biographical essay.

SV: In your most recent books you work with historical, referential material (Isaac Babel, your mother, and, more largely, your family, Emily Dickinson) but also on an autobiographical integration of this material.

147

JC: Yes, of course. If you look at *The Secret Life of Emily Dickinson*, I'm not trying to write a nineteenth-century novel. I'm trying to write a novel about Emily Dickinson as if she were in the twenty-first century. I'm not trying to mimic, to evaluate; I'm seeing her, basically, as a twenty-first-century creature trapped in her own time, and this was a means of getting her out of her time. One of the predicaments I had was that most scholars, when they talk about Emily Dickinson, really see her as someone who was very deprived, never left home, had no sexuality whatsoever. But it's a complete lie. She had a love affair in the last ten years of her life with her father's best friend; she wrote very sexual letters about this love affair. They're profoundly sexual. She wrote three letters to what she calls "the Master," which are very playful and very sexual at the same time. We have not only to reevaluate what her life was about, but to see her as a woman who lived a very profoundly rich life and was deprived of very, very little. The problem was, like most women, she wasn't able to work; she couldn't become a lawyer, she couldn't become a doctor, she couldn't get an education. She could either become a schoolmistress or get married. People ask: "Why didn't she marry?" There are no definite events that explain why she didn't marry. But the fact is that she was a huntress of language. She hunted in language in a way for which no other nineteenth-century writer in all of the English language was able to find any equivalent. She was so universally new in the way she saw language, in the way she played with language, that it's only now that we can really interpret what she was writing. It's so difficult to write about her. There's a dreadful play about Emily Dickinson called *The Belle of Amherst*, filled with clichés even though it's from her own voice. It's about this Emily Dickinson who supposedly never kissed a man, who was locked away in a kind of imprisonment. But she had an incredibly rich life! That's the distortion of historians. It's only now, in the last two or three years, that there have been interesting books where she's been reinterpreted in a very, very different way. Historians lie. The closer they remain to the truth, the more they lie because they cannot interpret with any kind of imagination. And the greatest sin of all: they have no language. And how can you write about someone who was all about language when you, yourself, have no language? There's a recent book by Brenda Wineapple which is a wonderful study about Emily Dickinson, written very beautifully. There have been other studies in the last five years, which move closer to the way I have interpreted Emily Dickinson. And I'm going to try to do the same for Abraham Lincoln.

RP: From her poetry it's easy enough to imagine the erotic dimension of her life. Was there an element of provocation in imagining the scene where she is in the tavern, for instance, or with the Judge? Were you trying in any way to provoke the reader?

JC: No, no, no! As far as the tavern is concerned, remember this is sort of a dreamscape, but all the material about Judge Lord you can find in her letters. The letters about Judge Lord are incredibly sexual, so we know that she did have a love affair with him. He had a stroke near the end of his life, so we don't know if he wanted to marry her, and I don't think she really wanted to marry him, but they certainly did have a love affair, so there's no imagination in that. As far as the tavern is concerned, it's fantasizing what it must have been like for any woman who couldn't go anywhere alone. If you went anywhere alone, you were a whore. You had to be accompanied. When we talk about Emily Dickinson being a recluse, we forget that when she had her dog, her Newfoundland, Carlo, she explored the entire town for ten years. She wasn't a recluse then at all, she went everywhere with Carlo. And it's only after Carlo dies, which is around 1866, that she becomes more and more reclusive, and she refers to Carlo as "my mute confederate." Thank God he couldn't talk back to her, I have to say!

When I was writing the novel I was trying to paint a dreamscape, to imagine how she must have felt, living in her own time with the realization that she was much, much brighter, brighter than all the men around her, brighter than anyone else in her hometown, except perhaps for her own sister-in-law, Susan. And what does a woman in the nineteenth century do when she is so intelligent, in a world that is so provincial? That's really the imprisonment of her predicament, I think.

RP: One of the images that emerges is that of the tiny Emily flying across the Commons with her dog. We hear about the dog in the letters and in some of the poems, but in the novel they become an infamous couple. How much of that is the imagination? Did you find pleasure in giving such a large role to the dog?

JC: We have to be a little bit careful here, because if you look at the historians, there are very, very few mentions of Carlo. If you look at her letters, there are at least five or six mentions of Carlo. We know historically that Carlo was a dog that was given to her by her father when he was traveling, so that if she was alone, he wanted her to have a dog. We do know that she had problems with her eyes, so in 1864–65 she made two trips to Cambridge without Carlo, and missed him very much. But it seems to me, if you understand what she says, that we can attest for the fact that she went for long walks every day with Carlo. By calling Carlo, in one of her letters, her "mute confederate," we can understand the role he had beside her. Remember she's tiny, and Carlo is enormous. There's no photograph of them together, but if you imagine them together, Carlo is probably almost as tall as she was. We don't know exactly how tall she was, I would say she was probably no taller than five feet one. We have one of her dresses, which gives us an idea of her height.

RP: I had reservations in the beginning about the idea of the novel. Everybody has "their" Emily Dickinson from reading the poems, but what I found extraordinary in the novel was the voice, or the voices, since she has different voices. How did you "get" those voices?

JC: The voice, of course, came through the reading and constant rereading of her letters. And the poems, of course, which I had already read, but the letters were essential. Remember, I'm not trying to mimic or simulate; I'm taking thirty, forty essential words or phrases, and I'm trying to use them in a way that will capture her essence without imitating her. I'm not a ventriloquist; I'm not a dummy standing there. She is Emily Dickinson as I see her, through the prism of the twenty-first century. It's interesting that you had qualms about writing about her in terms of a novel before reading. Why? Why would the idea of it disturb you?

RP: What I was more concerned about was . . .

JC: You almost felt it was a sacrilege, I assume.

RP: Yes, probably!

JC: Yes. Voilà. You see, this is what I'm left with. It happens with most people. The people who attacked me for doing the very same thing, not one of them had read the letters. Because once you read the letters, you see that there's a tremendous proximity between . . . And as a matter of fact, the professor who teaches the course on Emily Dickinson in Mount Holyoke (where she went for one year), said that my book was now his bible. Because it really allows him to understand what it must have been like for her to be at Mount Holyoke. Many people said, "How dare you take our precious Emily Dickinson in such a way?" Interestingly enough, very few of the poets could even read the book; they felt it was a violation. Even though (I have to confess that I say this with humility and arrogance at the same time) the poetry in my book is better than any of the poetry they've ever written in their books, it didn't make any difference. They felt threatened by someone writing a novel in her voice. And I find it very strange because if someone had said to me the same thing, I would be fascinated, I would be the first one to want to read it, to see the possibilities.

RP: I was enthralled once I read the book. What was the reception of the novel like? Critical because you transgressed taboos?
JC: Half the people I expected would react violently indeed hated it, and half the people just as violently loved it. And now, we have our own page on Facebook. It's enormously successful and we're getting more and more readers. It's a page that presents Emily Dickinson in the twenty-first century. People, of course, don't have to like the book. It's perfectly legitimate not to like it, but the arguments they used are completely silly, because it's 100 percent accurate to her life; everything that occurs in the book is accurate. Now, as to her visiting these inns, she probably wouldn't have, but other than that . . . In the very first page of the novel she falls in love with Tom, who's a handyman at Mount Holyoke. Well, if you see Tom as a kind of imagined ghost who will reappear in the rest of her life, and if you see Tom as part of her imagined world, then the landscape of the novel makes sense, but not if you try to read it in strictly realistic terms—how he appears in a circus, he's a thief in Cambridge, etc., etc. Every man she sees is an image of Tom. And even when she sees the handyman at the end of her life who isn't Tom, a handyman who dances with a cow, she tries to reimagine him as Tom too. I see the novel as a dream life.

SV: About the critical reception, do you have the impression that the attacks were more violent maybe because you chose a woman?
JC: Well, the attacks were all by women, not by men. Though those who loved it were also women. For example, Brenda Wineapple, who's written the most interesting book on Emily Dickinson, absolutely loved the book. She understood what I did. Those scholars who write about Emily Dickinson also understood. It was mainly those people who really hadn't read the letters who objected. The letters are every bit as brilliant as the poems themselves, in my opinion. They have the same genius. They're among the greatest letters ever written. She's playful; she wears a hundred different masks. They are extraordinary. They're not as experimental as the poems, but they're as brilliant.

Student 1: My problem is not about what happens to her in the book, but that the story is told by Emily Dickinson. You take her voice, and this feels strange to me.
JC: Why?

Student 1: Because her voice is hers. How could you take it?

JC: Well, what does any writer do but steal anyone else's voice? Let's take the logic of this argument. Whenever I deal with any character, I'm stealing this character's voice. I'm robbing that person of his or her voice, it's no different. So it seems a little bit strange to me that you would feel uncomfortable. You might try to feel the exact opposite: how wonderful it is for someone to dare, to try to grapple with what that voice means. I'm not suggesting how you should read the book, you're entitled to feel any way you want, but I would argue the fact that your claim, from my point of view, is not a legitimate one because every artist, every writer steals a voice in very much the same way. It's absolutely no different, whether the character is historical or imaginative, you're stealing their voice. In my own interpretation, when I'm writing this book, I become Emily Dickinson. And I have the right to become her. That would be my answer to your question. Your argument is legitimate, but I would counter it by saying that every art is a kind of theft, a kind of appropriation. I can tell you, it's not so easy to sustain a voice like that. When I say "I am Emily Dickinson," it's a different Emily Dickinson, of course. I'm not a ventriloquist.

Student 2: How do you relate to this young scholar who falls madly in love with Emily Dickinson in the book?

JC: [*Laughs*]. There was an older scholar who fell in love with her, in fact. There are so many falsifications, you see. People say she was utterly unknown in her lifetime, which isn't true. She had at least ten poems published, and the whole English department at Amherst College knew about her poems, and one of the professors knocked on her door and wanted to talk to her about her poems and she didn't want to. I would say that I'm being playful about this scholar who wants to appropriate her life, and you could also want to see him as myself if you wanted. I wouldn't know how to interpret that. But I think we have a very false image of what her life was like, even though I can't say what exactly her life was, but she was in her own time and town a very well-known poet. The argument "Did she want her poetry to be published?"—no one can answer that. No one really knows. We do know that she self-published her poems; she put them in booklets. When you do that, you're publishing your poems. There's no getting away from that. So she self-published her own poems, and we do know that there wasn't one single male critic, in her entire life, who had the slightest idea of what her poems were about, of what she was trying to do. And this is one of the predicaments. They said the rhythms were off, the poems were too rough; "spasmodic" was one of the words that they used. Higginson said the poems were "spasmodic." Isn't that what contemporary art is all about?

RP: You suggest that the poems were written for her father, and that the fascicles were constituted for him.

JC: That's only a theory, my point of view. I think that she had a lifelong love-hate affair with her father. She had an older brother, Austin, who was very sensitive when he was young, and who sort of grew out of his sensitivity, but when Austin wrote his college papers, her father compared them to Shakespeare and didn't even know that his own daughter was writing those extraordinary poems. I would say that the poems, to some degree, are a kind of dialogue with her father, even though her father is invisible in this dialogue. Again, it's only my interpretation. I would also assume that she didn't want to have her poems published, for whatever reason. Did she imagine that they would be published after she died? Could she possibly have known that she would become the great American poet? I have no idea. I think, in a strange way, she must have been very confident or she couldn't have written those poems. They are the art of someone who is absolutely confident in the work she's doing and confident in the aloneness of the work she's doing. She says, "These are my letters to the world," but letters that are never sent. We do know that some of her correspondence was burnt, but if you go back to the nineteenth century, most people got rid of correspondence when the person died, so that was not unusual. The most recent scholarship seems to conclude that her maid, Maggie, knew about the poems whereas her sister did not. We don't know how true this is, but there's been a very brilliant book published recently about Margaret Maher, the maid of the family, claiming that Emily Dickinson's poems were influenced by her. I would say that this is nonsense. In part they were influenced, but the argument is "Why were all these servants unknown?" and I would say Margaret Maher is only known because Emily Dickinson became a poet with a worldwide reputation, otherwise her maid would never be known! It works both ways. Her sister discovered her poems, the fascicles, in her drawer about a week after Emily died, didn't quite know what to do with them, and gave them to her sister-in-law, Susan. Susan was ambivalent in some way about the poems, wanted to publish them privately, so Emily's sister decided not to use Susan—but the finding of the poems was a very complicated matter and I don't want to go through it now. They were published about fifteen years after Emily Dickinson's death and they were reprinted almost immediately. Like Melville's works, they were only discovered as great poems in the 1920s, with the Renaissance of scholarship. In the 1920s, her profile suddenly exploded, we had all those interpretations about her life, and finally in the twenty-first century she becomes a cultural icon in the United States. We only have one photograph of her, taken when she was sixteen years old, a daguerreotype. She's really a twenty-first-century figure; she's more known now than she was in the twentieth century.

RP: In the writing of the novel did you discover an Emily Dickinson that you hadn't known and that emerged from progressive imagining?

JC: To put it in another way, I discovered my own female self. I wrote in a female voice. But did I discover another Emily Dickinson, I'm not sure. The real shock was reading the poems and the letters. That was the revelation. I can't say that there was a greater revelation beyond the discovery of her writings. A novel is a novel no matter what the subject is. It has its own finite shape, it has to move forward, and it has to have a kind of suspense and things that have nothing to do with Emily Dickinson. You have to be able to capture the form. A work is always about architecture and form, and how you fit the music into this form. That was the real predicament: how do you scope her life into a novel? The greatest pleasure I had was to reconstruct the poem "Because I could not stop for Death—/He kindly stopped for me," how I tried to reconstruct the carriage ride in the last three pages of the novel, when she's sort of floating her way towards the barn, which is a kind of haven. That is my favorite of all her poems, the poem I kept closest to.

RP: About the construction of the novel, the invention of the character Zilpah Marsh, she works as a kind of double for Emily?

JC: Yes, Zilpah Marsh is a young woman who goes to Mount Holyoke with Emily, but Zilpah comes from a very poor family, so she doesn't have a middle-class background, and therefore she suffers her entire life. I see her as a kind of shadow creature. If you look at Doctor Jekyll and Mister Hyde, if you try to see Emily in Zilpah—Zilpah is Emily taken outside of civilization. I could not have written this novel with the same power without this character. To me, Zilpah is the most important character in the book, as important as Emily. Zilpah ends up in an insane asylum, and there's a very long scene when Emily and her father visit her in this asylum.

SV: What is the exact function of the "Author's Note" you use as an introduction to the novel? Of course, you explain the project of the novel, what you wanted to do, and you use this expression "my Emily."

JC: You see, I'm trying to answer your questions by putting an author's note to say that I do this with a great deal of humility, that to me if I was going to write a novel about Emily Dickinson, there was no other way but to write it in her own voice. And I'm doing the same with Lincoln now. Maybe it won't work. I hope it will! I couldn't have gotten into the text, because as I said music is the most critical apparatus, and I couldn't have found the music without getting into her voice. I needed this introduction.

SV: And also at the beginning of the introduction, you briefly evoke your very first discovery of Emily Dickinson, when you were still extremely young.
JC: Yes, she was the first poet that I discovered, and she was very, very important to me, as a child. When I discovered the poem "Success is counted sweetest," I didn't even know who the author was. It talks about failure and the right and the pride of failure, and also the necessity of failure: to succeed, one does have to fail. I couldn't have done this novel ten years earlier. I think I wouldn't have had the equilibrium to have done it when I was much younger. When I finally wrote the novel, I was willing to fail. I was willing to take the risk of it not working out.

SV: But in a way, this introduction resembles the beginning of the book on Isaac Babel, in which you also explain that you went through a revelation when you discovered him. Babel's short stories, Emily Dickinson's poems . . .
JC: Yes, it's practically the same book!

SV: Exactly.
JC: *Savage Shorthand* is a book about Isaac Babel and this is a book about Emily Dickinson, but they are my dialogues with Babel and Emily Dickinson, my talking to them.

SV: And also, Babel even today is still a very mysterious man, with a mysterious life, a mysterious death too: there was this fiction about Babel being sent to a camp for years, a fiction created by the NKVD that refused to admit they had shot him.
JC: Yes, it was only in 1954, when the KGB files were opened up, that we discovered that he died in 1940 or '41. He was shot right in the Loubianka. There was no reason in the world to kill him. It was a completely satanic act which doesn't make any sense.

SV: But in a way Babel and Emily Dickinson both are—and this is perhaps why so many "specialists" attacked you in both cases—embodiments of ultimate mystery. If you had decided to write a novel about Whitman, for instance, I'm not sure the result would have been the same as far as reception is concerned.

JC: But I wouldn't have written a book about Walt Whitman.

SV: [*Laughs*] Yes, what I mean is that in both cases you destroyed myths that people like to cling to.

JC: Yes, but I also think that they're wrong. Even though a book has to find its own reception, and I'm not going to try and say what the reception of these books will be, I still think those critics were wrong. The book on Babel tells more about Babel through telling about myself than a very, very strict biography which tells you nothing. If you want to go out to the very edge, you have to be willing to suffer to be there and to stay at the edge. Many people loved the book and understood it, other people didn't.

SV: A lot of criticisms came from the fact that your voice is so mixed with Babel's voice, or imaginary voice, or reinvented voice, that it becomes disturbing for people. It's like one voice.

JC: It's only disturbing if they're not willing to go on that adventure. The adventure is a kind of induced schizophrenia when you don't know where you are, where you cannot locate yourself, and to me, the greatest of all books approach a kind of madness. They don't take you into madness, but get as close to it as possible. To derangement. You lose yourself before you find what's in the book. At least when I read Emily Dickinson for the first time, that's exactly how I felt. I didn't know who I was in relation to the poems that I was reading. They were so extraordinary, so unlike anything I had ever read, that I could not locate myself in relation to them. That's what startled me. When I read, for example, *Lolita* for the first time, and just the opening, "Lo-lee-ta, three tips of the tongue," there was something so musical about that book; it's so close to hallucination and so close to madness. The character of Quilty is the writer. Quilty is Nabokov in some way, the ventriloquist assuming all these voices. The notion of madness, of approaching madness, of getting as close to chaos as you can. In *War Cries over Avenue C*, I think I did that; I couldn't really go beyond that point and remain sane. That's as far as I could go, and from that point on, I began to withdraw into more conventional works because I couldn't go any further. I would have had to lose myself in the text.

Student 2: I find this idea of losing yourself very interesting. When you read novels, do you try and find the author behind the text?

JC: No, I never search for the author; I only search for the text. It's very hard for me to read, because I have to find the music. Writing a book is about the music, it's about the voice. This is what predominates. The music is all, the music is total, it's absolute, and in the case of Dickinson it's two centuries ahead of her own time. It's even hard to understand some of the slides that she makes with her dash even now, because she's so far in advance of her own time. And those critics who like to tie her to her own time don't really understand the quality of her genius. Her genius is outside of time itself. And if you look at other writers like Melville, Shakespeare, or Dickens, that's always the same: the music doesn't bear any witness, even though those writers are writing about their own time; if Melville is writing about the *Pequod* and compares it to capitalism in the nineteenth century, he's still writing about something that is so distant inside his head that even now we cannot interpret novels such as *The Confidence Man*, we don't have the equipment, psychologically, to understand the way his mind was working. Maybe some of you will disagree. I find the music in Wallace Stevens, in Yeats, in James Joyce, and I particularly find it in William Faulkner. In modern writers it's very difficult for me to find any music. For example, if you look at early Saul Bellow, *The Adventures of Augie March*, I do find the music there, but I don't find the music at all in his later novels. I'm searching for the text, not the persona behind the text.

Student 2: Was Emily Dickinson an exception then?

JC: No, she wasn't an exception because first of all, when you grow up you have a certain chauvinism about males—all the writers are males, so how can a female be a writer, you know, that kind of chauvinistic clichés. So when you discover a writer like Emily Dickinson who's greater than all the male writers that you know, suddenly your landscape has to change and after a while, you begin to read about her and her persona, but for a very long time, I didn't know anything about her other than her poems. It's only later that I began to really get into the discourse about her life and I didn't find that discourse very interesting. The novel, to me, is about the celebration of her language, whether it's in the poetry or in the letters. I'm celebrating her language in my own way, and I did the same thing with Isaac Babel, I think.

Student 2: I find your approach to books as "adventures" very interesting.

You seem to be very interested in myths, popular myths, and also in history. It evokes Ken Burns to me.

JC: Yes, a little bit, and also I should say that the first book I read was *Pinocchio*, so that in some sense all the books I write are almost a child's adventures in the world. If you look at some of the adventures Emily goes through in Cambridge—she could be Pinocchio in "The Land of Bad Boys." It's pretty much the same thing. It's myths and history. I find it very difficult to deal with the future, to write science fiction, for example. I cannot find a science fiction text where the language holds me. There are science fiction films, *Blade Runner* for example, that are great films, but when I read the novel the movie is based on, I didn't find it interesting at all. Cinema is very important in the writing of most of my books, because they could almost be seen as composed the way scenes are in a film, the cutting, you know, from scene to scene. Both comic books and cinema are very important in these texts. And also they're texts that explode and that take you in a kind of quicksand where you don't know where you are, at some point. Maybe that's one reason why readers have difficulty with some of the books, because no one is holding your hand. You're there alone. Of course that's the way I like to read.

SV: In some of your interviews you've often said that because you started reading comic books when you were young, in a way your reading education was based on these images and frames, and then when you started to work on *bandes dessinées* with different artists you could find again this way of looking at a story. When you mentioned, earlier in this discussion, the way Emily Dickinson uses dashes, which you call 'slides,' I was wondering whether you could make a link between this way you have of cutting your stories and sentences, which is very special, and her writing.

JC: I think the dash that she uses, the ellipses when she goes from image to image would be like going from panel to panel in a comic book. Her use of the dash is very violent, very violent. She's much more violent than any other writer, and also very wicked, very playful and very wicked. There is one line in which she talks about being married, "Born—Bridalled—Shrouded." She can go through an entire life with three words. You have to be absolutely brilliant to have this kind of shorthand, and it's the same shorthand that Isaac Babel has. To suddenly deal with language as if it was a kind of telegraph, where you just . . . The verbs, you know, the great writers would take the verbs and use them as adjectives. They would take the verbs and use them in a way other writers can't, and you can see that in Dickens and Shakespeare. How could there be such a person as Shakespeare? There are so many theories about whether he learnt Latin or not, whether he went to school or didn't. We don't know the first thing about him. All we know is that we have these brilliant texts and there are no equivalents in all of the English language. When Hamlet describes a cloud that looks like a camel's back and the permutation of things, he's not only our contemporary, he's so far ahead of us. I feel the same way about Emily Dickinson, about Nabokov. They just understand language in ways that we don't, that we aren't equipped to do, it seems to me.

RP: I have an anecdotal question: you write a lot about her red hair, her father's hair. It comes back all the time.
JC: [*Laughs*] I must say I was very attracted to red heads as a child! Red hair to me was almost magical, somehow. I don't know why, freckles and red hair. She had a freckled face with red hair. She wasn't particularly attractive, she had an overbite. Redness in terms of flame, in terms of fire, and emotions—I wouldn't say passion, I would say emotion—is very important. It gave me a chance to play with the word fire. Fire is very important because as you burn up, you also are renewed. In one sense, one has to die and be reborn in a text, and that's not so easy to do. You have to go through a kind of death to go to the other side, it seems to me. In the text, I'm only talking about the text.

RP: It's a very beautiful book. Did you participate in the choices that were made?
JC: It's thanks to the editor. The two books I did with them (*Johnny One-Eye* and *The Secret Life of Emily Dickinson*) . . . I've done a book on Joe DiMaggio which will be out next fall, and we now have a new law in the U.S. where the owner of the copyright also owns the copyright of the image; it doesn't matter who is taking the photograph. In other words, if you want to publish a photograph of Marilyn Monroe, you have to get the permission of the estate to do it. They own the copyright of the image. In this case, it's a little bit different: the owners of the images I used are generally Harvard University Press. It was very, very hard to get them. The one I like best is the one of her dress. That was really curious: it was really like going through a maze. I think the Emily Dickinson museum took the photograph of her dress, but didn't own the right to the photograph. Nobody seemed to know who owned the rights to the photograph. They said, "We have the rights to the photograph but not to her dress." Finally we published it. The publisher did a very beautiful book, which is very rare today. I was very lucky that they

paid such attention to the paper, the rough paper. Still they wouldn't do certain things. To me, colored end-papers are very important. The end-papers should be colored. When they're not, it really bothers me. But in order to have them colored, you have to sell a lot of books! If I was able to sell a hundred thousand copies of a book, I wouldn't negotiate in terms of money, I would be able to demand a cloth cover and not a cardboard cover, colored end-papers, and these are things that are difficult to obtain. But I would say that they did as beautiful a book as one could possibly do in 2010 when most books look terrible. You have to fight for everything.

RP: Has it sold very well?
JC: It sold okay. It hasn't sold as well as they would have liked to have sold it. It's coming out in French; Rivages will be publishing it, and it will come out in paperback also.

SV: One last question about Emily Dickinson: you said you wouldn't have been able to write the book ten years earlier, and I was wondering . . . I remember reading an interview dating back to the 1990s, and the question was about women in your work, and although I disagreed about what the journalist was saying, he said something about women characters in your work who were not that numerous and that developed, and you answered that you were writing a book about your mother (*The Dark Lady from Belorusse*), so maybe it was going to change.
JC: Yes, perhaps it was after the death of my mother. It's very difficult to write about your mother as a sexual person. It's hard to enter your mother's bedroom' it's a kind of violation. But somehow, after she died, I could see her in sexual terms, which I hadn't been able to do during her lifetime. My mother was very, very beautiful when she was young. I remember walking down the street with her and people couldn't take their eyes off her. She had this Russian look. She never smiled. She just had this power. Beauty is a kind of power, it seems to me. So it was only after she died that I was able to write about her.

SV: You reinvented your mother in *The Dark Lady*.
JC: Of course, she becomes a fictional character.

SV: Yes, but I have the impression that what you did with Emily Dickinson was possible after the incredible reinvention of Fanny.
JC: Yes, that's probably true.

Index

Abish, Walter, 89, 111

Actors Studio, 5, 24–25

Anderson, Sherwood, 78

Arnold, Benedict, 115, 124

Auster, Paul, 91, 142–43

autobiography/autobiographical novels, 118–20, 126, 128–31, 134–37, 140, 142, 147

Babel, Isaac, xiv, 106–7, 116, 119, 122, 125, 126, 141, 145, 155–56, 158

Balzac, Honoré de, 30, 33

Bambi, 96, 141

Barthelme, Donald, 57, 59, 60, 63, 66, 68, 108, 113

Barthes, Roland, 57, 80

baseball, 6, 36–37, 62

Baudelaire, Charles, 36, 115, 128

Beckett, Samuel, 36

Bellow, Saul, 133, 157

Benacquista, Tonino, 104

biography/biographical novels, 120–21, 125, 147, 156

Borges, Jorge Luis, 36

Boucq, François, xi, 24, 104

Bowles, Paul, 19

Brecht, Bertolt, 36

Bronx, xiii, 10, 12–13, 17–18, 26, 54, 70, 110–12, 114, 116, 131–32, 145; Crotona Park, 40, 41; Morrisania, 26

brotherhood, 139–40

Burroughs, William, 23

Calvino, Italo, 36

Céline, Louis-Ferdinand, 105

Chandler, Raymond, 30, 36

chaos, 33, 36–37, 75–77, 98

characters, 19, 30–31, 55, 78, 99; Isaac Sidel, xi, xv, 8, 9, 11, 22, 30, 32–33, 51, 72, 73–77, 79, 82, 83, 99, 100, 103, 109, 118, 125, 130, 137–39; Jeronimo, 78; Manfred Coen, xi, xiv, 9, 22, 73, 82, 109, 130, 137–38; Marilyn the Wild, xi, 18, 138; Sidney Holden, 10, 35, 84, 99, 128, 138; women, 18, 100–101

Charyn, Jerome: academic education, 52, 71, 144; awkwardness, 11–12; brother (Harvey), xiii, 12–14, 46–48, 51, 53–54, 73, 87, 109, 112, 125, 129–30, 137, 139, 142; brother (Marvin), 140; career, xv, 72; childhood, xii, xiv, 118, 122; family, 11, 101–2, 137; father, xii, xiii, 14, 27, 34, 44–45, 101, 134, 136, 140–41, 143–45; marriage, 11, 20, 136–37; mother, xii, xiii, 11, 18, 27, 34, 55, 101, 122, 123–24, 134, 135–37, 160; mother tongue, 27, 34, 133–34; parents, 27, 39, 70, 103, 137

Autobiographical volumes: *The Black Swan*, xiii, 118, 135; *Bronx Boy,* xiii, 118, 135; *The Dark Lady from Belorusse*, xiii, 118, 122, 123, 128, 129, 134–37, 147, 160

Crime fiction: *Arnold, le geek de New York*, 30; *Blue Eyes*, xii, 9, 22, 30, 54, 79, 87, 91, 100, 109, 125; *Death of a Tango King*, 58; *The Education of Patrick Silver*, 22, 41, 100; *Elsinore*, 9, 14, 35, 99; *The Good Policeman*, 8, 48–49, 108; *Maria's Girls*, 109; *Marilyn the Wild*, 18, 22, 41, 54, 100; *Montezuma's Man*, 81, 83; *Paradise Man*, 9–10, 14–16, 18, 25, 41, 99, 128; *Secret Isaac*, 22, 73, 76, 79–80, 90, 100, 129

Fiction: *American Scrapbook*, 21, 129; *The Catfish Man*, 6, 35, 118, 120, 129, 139, 140, 145; *Darlin' Bill*, 101, 128; *Eisenhower, My Eisenhower*, xii, 20–21, 41, 43, 64, 67, 72–73, 107, 123; *The Franklin Scare*, 22, 125; *Going to Jerusalem*, 21; *The Green Lantern*, 111, 116–17, 124; *Jerzy Kosinsky*, xiv, 121, 124; *Johnny One-Eye*, 118, 124, 125, 142, 159; *Once upon a Droshky*, 8, 21, 72, 106, 123; *On the Darkening Green*, 123; *Panna Maria*, xiii, 18, 19–20, 101–2; *Pinocchio's Nose*, xiii, 6, 8, 57–58, 87, 108, 120, 129, 142; *The Secret Life of Emily Dickinson*, xiv, 118–19, 123, 125–26, 127, 131, 148–60; *The Seventh Babe*, 6; *The Tar Baby*, 21, 108, 124; *War Cries over Avenue C*, 6, 20, 99, 128, 156

Graphic novel, *The Magician's Wife*, 3–4, 7, 24

Nonfiction: *Metropolis*, xiii, 26, 29, 30, 39–49, 73; *Movieland*, 28, 108; *Savage Shorthand*, xiv, 119–20, 125, 141, 145, 155

Paratexts: "Harvey," 118, 129–30; "Jerome Charyn" in *Contemporary Authors' Autobiography Series*, 118, 126, 141

Play, *George*, 7, 25, 33

Short stories: "Faigele the Idiotke," 8, 106, 127; "The Man Who Grew Younger," 9; "1944," 36, 142

Short story collection, *The Man Who Grew Younger*, 36, 142, 144

Chénetier, Marc, xi, 101

chess, 36–37

Cohen, Leonard, 108

comic books/graphic novels/*bande dessinée*, xii, 3–7, 13–14, 16–17, 24, 28, 35, 39, 56, 70, 103–4, 109, 114, 158

Conrad, Joseph, 75, 83–84

Cooper, Gary, 28, 49

crime fiction/detective fiction, 14, 22, 36, 73, 79–80, 87–89, 93–95, 109; constraints of, 89–91; French *polar*, xii, xvi, 56, 97, 103–4

Daeninckx, Didier, 104

Deleuze, Gilles, 139, 146

DeLillo, Don, 113, 131–32

Dickens, Charles, 28, 78, 158

Dickinson, Emily, xiv, 119, 120, 125–26, 127, 132, 139, 146, 148–60

DiMaggio, Joe, 125, 147, 159

Dostoevsky, Fyodor, 36, 78, 111

Duhamel, Marcel, xi

Elkin, Stanley, 23, 61, 108

Ellis Island, xiii, 19, 32, 39–41

Euripides, 96

fantasy, 6, 19, 42, 109

father and son relationship, 82–83, 91–92, 137–38

Faulkner, William, xiv, xv, 10, 21, 36, 52, 57, 58, 60, 61, 65, 69, 73, 77–78, 84, 90, 93, 111, 112, 114, 120, 121, 122, 157

film/movies, 5, 10, 28–29, 35, 47, 48–49, 95–96, 114, 158; *The Big Sleep*, 6; *Blade Runner*, 158; *The Curious Case of Benjamin Button*, 140; documentaries, 44, 47; *Duck Soup*, 6; film noir, xiv, 95–96; *The Lady from Shangai*, 76; *Pépé le Moko*, 50; *Prizzi's Honor*, 6, 9–11; *Public Enemy*, 29; *Pulp Fiction*, 85–86, 113; *Récits d'Ellis Island*, 38, 40; *Route One/USA*, 39; *Sea of Love*, 10; *Singin' in the Rain*, 29; *T-Men*, 96

Flaubert, Gustave, 128

Freud, Sigmund, 53

gangster, xiv, 10, 29, 52, 80; gangster-writer, xiv, 52, 80

García Márquez, Gabriel, *One Hundred Years of Solitude*, 10, 94

Gass, William, xv, 23, 59, 61, 67, 69, 83, 84, 92, 113, 120, 121, 122, 126

geek, 14, 30, 32, 51, 78

Genet, Jean, xiv, 105

Ginsberg, Allen, 20

golem, xiii, 26, 32–33, 71–72

Gould, Glenn, 120, 127

Griffith, D. W., 48

grotesque, 78

guilt, 33, 34, 71, 74, 82

Hammett, Dashiell, xii, xv, 36, 79, 88–89, 90

Hawkes, John, xv, 60, 61, 65, 67, 68, 88, 93, 107

Hawthorne, Nathaniel, 132–33

Hemingway, Ernest, xiv, 10, 65, 111, 113, 121

Herriman, George, *Krazy Kat*, 5, 20, 61

Himes, Chester, 36

idiot/idiot savant, 8–9, 11, 12, 13, 25, 60, 106, 127, 140

immigrants/immigration, 11, 19, 27, 29, 34–35, 40–41, 43, 46, 55

intertext, 66, 76, 85, 86, 121–22

James, Henry, 21, 35, 133

Jews/Jewishness, 11, 13, 19, 30, 32, 41, 43, 102, 103, 117, 123, 131, 136, 138, 144, 145

Joyce, James, xv, 34, 53, 58, 73, 76, 90, 120, 122, 137, 157

Kafka, Franz, 71

Koch, Ed, 31–32, 40, 48, 73

Kosinsky, Jerzy, 121

Kramer, Robert, 39

Lang, Fritz, 45

language, xv, 27–28, 34, 36, 44–45, 57–69, 71, 76–77, 80–83, 84, 87–88, 91–92, 95, 107, 115, 134, 146; absence of, xv, 27, 34, 39, 44–45, 52, 56, 70, 95, 127, 140, 142; French, 56, 104–5; 115; music of, xv, 57–58, 59–60, 65–67, 72–73, 83, 85, 91–92, 120, 126, 129, 157; violence/cruelty of, 80–81, 88, 158

Loustal, Jacques de, 7–8, 17, 86, 104

Mafia, 31, 46–47, 53–54, 74, 98

Malamud, Bernard, 94

McCarthy, Cormac, 120, 126

Melville, Herman, xv, 21, 35–36, 60, 64, 93, 106, 127, 132–33, 139, 157

Modiano, Patrick, 127–28

Monroe, Marilyn, 121, 129, 159

Muñoz, José, 109
Muñoz, Juan, 104
Mussolini, Benito, 108, 142, 143
mythologization, xiii, 62, 64, 128, 135
mythology: American, 92; immigrant, 41, 43; New York, 33, 45–46; personal, xiv–xv, 55–56, 72, 135, 140
mythopsychosis, xiii, 57–58, 62, 64

Nabokov, Vladimir, xv, 21, 34, 58, 61, 90, 107, 113, 120, 121, 126, 133, 134, 156
New York, xiii, xv, 27, 31–32, 33, 39, 42–46, 50–51, 54–55, 73, 75, 97, 102–3, 106, 124, 131
nonfiction, 129, 147

Oates, Joyce Carol, 89–90, 134
Ozick, Cynthia, 59

Paley, Grace, 23, 59, 113
paratext/peritext, 118, 125, 129–30, 155
Paris, xiii, xv, 24, 27, 37, 50–51, 56, 98, 110, 115, 124, 131
Penn, Arthur, 16, 25
Pennac, Daniel, 104–5
Perec, Georges, and Robert Bober, *Récits d'Ellis Island*, 38, 40
Ping-Pong, 36–37, 53, 110
Pinocchio (Carlo Collodi), xiii, 35, 62, 87, 96, 141–46, 158
Pinter, Harold, 82
Preminger, Otto, 15–16
Pynchon, Thomas, 57, 63, 67

reader, 28, 52, 75–76, 81, 83, 102
realism, 5–6, 20, 114, 120, 151
reception, 6–7, 20–22, 25, 109, 119, 120, 125–26, 151
Rimbaud, Arthur, 36, 104, 115, 128

Salinger, J. D., 84, 134
screenwriting, 7, 15–16, 29
Shakespeare, William, 157, 158–59
Singer, Isaac Bashevis, 36, 106–7
solitude/aloneness of the writer, 35, 122, 130–31, 153
Sophocles, 10, 71, 96
Spinoza, Barch, 30
Stalin, Joseph, 52, 111, 116, 124, 138
Stanford University, 20, 60, 88, 108
Stevens, Wallace, 157
style, xii, 43, 44, 63, 79

teaching, 20, 23
translation, 25, 101, 105, 135
Tuten, Frederic, 23, 113, 116, 117

undersong, xii, 58, 62, 64, 75

voice, xii, xiv, xv, 20–21, 28, 50, 51, 52, 57, 59, 60–69, 99, 107, 108, 118–19, 121–22, 123, 125, 127, 130, 135, 144, 146, 150–52, 154–55, 156, 157
Voice Project, 60, 88, 108

walking, 18, 27, 37
Washington, George, 115, 118, 142
writing, xii, xvi, 8, 11, 12, 23, 35, 52–53, 58–59, 65–66, 70–71, 80, 81, 85, 93, 103, 122, 145, 146, 157

Yeats, William Butler, 157
Yiddish, 27, 34, 133

Printed in the United States
by Baker & Taylor Publisher Services